fiona horne's guide to coven magick

Fiona Horne is the author of eight books on Witchcraft. A television presenter/producer, radio personality, and actress, she has been a practicing Witch for nineteen years. In late 2001, Fiona moved to America to further pursue her career in television and publishing. At the same time, she formed her coven, the Dark Light of Lilith Coven, and is now casting her spell over Hollywood. To find out more, visit www.fionahorne.com.

Also by Fiona Horne

Witch: A Magickal Journey (Thorsons/Harper Collins, 2001)

Witchin': A Handbook for Teen Witches (Thorsons/Element/Harper Collins, 2003)

7 Days to a Magickal New You (Thorsons/Harper Collins, 2003)

Magickal Sex: A Witch's Guide to Beds, Knobs and Broomsticks (Thorsons/Harper Collins, 2003)

POP! Goes the Witch: The Disinformation Guide to 21st Century Witchcraft (Disinformation, 2004)

Bewitch a Man (Simon Spotlight/Simon & Schuster, 2006)

FIONA HORNE

LA

fiona horne's guide to coven magick

Witch

Llewellyn Publications
Woodbury, Minnesota

SECOND EDITION
First Printing, 2007

This book was previously published in 2003 by Random House Australia
under the title *The Coven: Making Magick Together*

Book design by Rebecca Zins

Cover design by Kevin R. Brown

Cover photos: top © Rubberball Productions, John Wang; bottom © Photodisc

Llewellyn is a registered trademark of Llewellyn Worldwide, Ltd.

The Cataloging-in-Publication Data for *L.A. Witch* is on file at the Library of Congress.
ISBN-13: 978-0-7387-1034-1
ISBN-10: 0-7387-1034-2

Llewellyn Publications
A Division of Llewellyn Worldwide, Ltd.
2143 Wooddale Drive, Dept. 0-7387-1034-2
Woodbury, MN 55125-2989, U.S.A.
www.llewellyn.com

Printed in the United States of America

To my gorgeous sisters of the Dark Light of Lilith Coven, Tri and Zorrita, and to all the L.A. witchy women who join me for open magickal meetings and goddess gatherings!

To Bill and Antonia Beattie, thank you for giving me a good push in the right direction when I needed it and indispensable advice and assistance.

To my dear friends and family who have encouraged me and supported me through the last five intense years.

To my fabulously creative team at fionahorne.com: Josh Bouman and Andrew Stopps.

Love and thanks to Tri Johns, Ally Peltier, Serene Conneeley, and Dylan Masson for sharing their personal stories in this book.

And finally a special thanks to the ocean and the sky. As a scuba diver of over twenty years and now a sky diver of over twenty jumps (and counting!), I am continually astounded by the magnificence of life and feel deeply blessed to be alive in these extraordinary times on this beautiful, divine planet. And we all know modern witches don't fly on broomsticks and float on water—we jump out of planes and scuba dive!

Blessed be.

Contents

me, you . . . a coven?   1

what a witch is   9

covencrafting   25

bring it on   35

let's get going   47

rite now!   57

dedicate your coven   79

making magick together   95

goddess gatherings   111

share the love   123

how spells work   137

hey, this is fun!   143

room for improvement   149

you sexy witch!   159

questions from the forum   163

homework   171

witchcraft 101   185

reaching out   193

appendices

the elements of me by tri johns

201

living and loving it by allyson e. peltier

207

serene serene by serene conneeley

213

coven sutra by dylan masson

219

websites & contacts

225

recommended reading

229

Me, You . . . a Coven?

Hello there. It occurs to me that, even though I have written many books on Witchcraft that have been released around the world over the last seven years, this may be the first time some of you and I have met. So it feels right to tell you a bit about myself and explain what brought me here—an Aussie Witch living in Los Angeles!

I have been a practicing Witch for nineteen years. During part of that time, I sang in an Australian electronic rock group called Def FX. For seven years, we released successful albums and toured Australia and America many times, both as a headlining act and playing alongside bands like No Doubt, the Smashing Pumpkins, Soundgarden, and the Beastie Boys.

MTV played our videos, we were on the Billboard charts, and we were carving out quite a nice career for ourselves until we broke up in a rather untimely fashion. The aftermath was a really sad and difficult time for me. During my career with the band I had been practicing Witchcraft, but I never came out about it publicly, apart from wearing my pentagram necklace on a couple of CD covers. My song lyrics did suggest my esoteric interests and I was pretty wild and free onstage, but that was about as magickal as I let the public know my life was. So, when the band ended, part of the healing process involved me "coming out of the broom closet," so to speak. I wrote a book. At the same time, the performer in me still needed an outlet to let off creative steam, so I started to channel all the energy from my onstage performances directly into working in television and radio, as well as writing.

My first book, *Witch: A Magickal Journey*, created quite a splash in America (though I had been an "out" Witch for a number of years previously in Australia), partly because I work in the entertainment industry and I am very open about my spirituality. Coming out as a Witch has helped to open a lot of people's eyes as to what modern Witchcraft is and isn't, and I think it has helped to dispel a lot of the negative stereotypes associated with the Craft. I also started hosting my own television show and appearing on a popular morning radio show providing "magickal solutions" for call-in listeners—that is, I prescribed spells (augmented with some practical advice) for everyday dilemmas.

I began to find that what had once been an intensely private spiritual pursuit started to blend strongly with my career. I grappled with this for a while, wondering if it was appropriate to be so open about what is essentially an occult spiritual tradition (by dictionary definition, *occult* means "hidden and secret"). I wondered whether I was contributing to the dissolution of its essence—making it too available and even perhaps trivializing it.

But my concerns were quashed as I received more and more positive feedback from both the Pagan and the Craft communities and newcomers who were applauding my efforts in opening up access to spiritual knowledge that people wanted and even needed.

At the same time, a proliferation of books started to appear, and soon Wicca/Witchcraft was being credited as the fastest-growing spiritual path in the Western world. The more lectures and appearances I did in America and on trips to the United Kingdom as my books were released there, the more Witches—both old and new—I met. This made me realize that what I am doing (along with other "out" public Witches) is contributing to a positive phase of spiritual evolution. And a big part of doing this means embracing modern methods of communication and expression. If Jesus were around now, he would probably have his own TV show, his own website, and a series of books. It's all just a sign of the times.

And so I stopped holding back and decided to dive right in and really let my career and spirituality fuel and enhance each other. I decided I wanted to see how far I could go and how much good I could do. In saying this, I am certainly not on a crusade to convert the Western world to Witchcraft, but I do want to help people feel good about themselves, and I do want to help people feel happy and fulfilled. Sharing my experiences about life as a Witch in my books and being prepared to answer questions and provide reliable information on the Craft is a way for me to do that.

Moving to America was a huge step for me. Australia is a beautiful, uncrowded, geographically isolated, easy place to reside. By contrast, America is a challenging and confronting environment. The country is also unique in the way it welcomes immigrants—especially if you work in the arts. I have found America is a country of phenomenal opportunity if you are prepared to work hard and can stay focused and committed to the task.

However, it was a pretty big deal to decide to pack up my comfortable life in Australia and make the move to the overwhelming and monolithic United States of America. I think that if I'd had any inkling of how hard it was really going to be I probably never would have left. But I felt drawn to America, and not just because of dreams and goals I'd had since I was a young girl wanting to live a "large life" but by something far more subtle and profound. It just felt right and was something I had to do.

The day I rocked up to L.A., I had to pretty much start again from scratch. It was like establishing a new identity: I had no rental history, no credit—nothing. I didn't even have a driver's license (I only started to drive when I moved to Los Angeles—before that a taxi or a broomstick was good enough!). But now, a few years down the road, I've got a good home, great friends, a growing career, and I feel happy and fulfilled.

For most of my witchy life I have been solitary—that is, practicing the Craft on my own, not as part of a coven. Initially it was really hard to find reliable information about the Craft. When I started out there weren't many books, certainly not published in Australia, explaining how to do things "Down Under." (For example, all the books written in the Northern Hemisphere had northern dates for festivals like Yule, the Winter Solstice, which is approximately December 22.

In Australia, December 22 is the middle of summer!) There was no Internet, so no chat rooms or websites to gain information and connect with people. In the 1980s there was still also the ingrained stigma that Witches were Satanic and evil (fortunately this has eroded significantly now) or that they were fantasy figures and "imaginary."

So in my early witchy years, I kept my path quiet. Anyway, I enjoyed being solitary. It gave me room to develop at my own pace and, to be honest, some of the people I did cross paths with who claimed they were Witches seemed more like wankers! The last thing I wanted to do was associate myself with them.

After a number of years, I reached a point where I had accumulated a lot of knowledge, and I was very comfortable with circlecasting and conjuring, solitary sabbat celebrations, and full moon rituals. I could really concentrate on making my actions magickal as well as practical. That is, I could let go of worrying about doing it properly or by the current book I was reading and trust in my own intuition. I was perfectly happy with my craft.

So why did I decide to leave this utopian, solo witchy existence and unveil my innermost magickal self to others by deciding to form a coven? I think a big part of this was triggered by my move to Los Angeles.

Anyone who has lived in Hollywood will know that it's a place built on dreams—and most of them are broken. Sometimes you can literally smell the desperation in the streets. In my first couple of years here I was led down every garden path imaginable, both professionally and personally. But I learned that you have to be very, very patient and not take the insincerity and lies personally, and you need to surround yourself with people who motivate and support you (it's the same anywhere, but particularly here in "the Dream Factory"). As I struggled to find my feet in this town, I felt more and more that perhaps I needed a support group, people who were on the same wavelength and who weren't a part of this cracked, fractured, materialistic, and shallow entertainment industry. I knew I needed to take action to nurture and protect my spiritual self. So I decided to put it out to the universe that I wanted to meet other Witches with whom I could form a coven.

I was conducting a workshop on Witchcraft at the renowned Bodhi Tree Bookstore on Melrose when I met Tri, my first covener. I have conducted many workshops and met many, many people, but Tri really stood out to me. We exchanged phone numbers and over a few months forged a friendship, eventually deciding to form a coven together. Tri then brought our next covener into the fold: a girlfriend of hers, Zorrita. Zorrita isn't a Witch but she is very spiritual and well versed in Mayan and Santerian magick. Tri and I knew that she would fit in perfectly and learn as much from us as we would from her. We three are now a coven.

I am now known to the Pagan community here and participate in festivals and events, and am invited to appear on television and radio shows to talk about Witchcraft and demonstrate spellcasting. Like I said before, I'm not on a mission to convert people—that's the last thing I want to do; if there's one thing all varieties of Witches have in common, it's that we don't proselytize. But as a performer by trade, if I can fulfill my creative expression and effect some positive change in the world, then it's all good!

Having kept my craft in the broom closet for so long, it feels like a natural extension of my evolution as a Witch to share what I know with those who ask for it. Especially with my coven sisters . . . and I must say that I am honored when they share their knowledge and insights with me in return!

As I receive more and more public exposure, I am increasingly approached by people who need help. It has snowballed a bit since the word is out that I can also do spells for people that really work. I don't advertise, of course—the interest is generated only by word of mouth (up until writing about it in this book!) and I don't charge money for my services. When the spell works, I ask the recipient to donate money to charity or to do something good for the community in order to share their success and good fortune with others; to pay it forward, so to speak. So it seems like every week I am heading out to houses in the Hollywood Hills that won't sell and performing cleansing rituals, or I'm down at the beach helping a jilted lover cast their unhappy past into the healing ocean so that they can move on and experience new and more fulfilling love. At the other, more bizarre, end of the surreal Hollywood spectrum, I was once asked to do an unhexing spell for a very well-known film director and a high-profile record producer, as a huge recording star had allegedly paid a Voodoo priest to do a death curse on both of them! I rarely turn people down, but sometimes I know that the best way to help is by encouraging the person to deal with the difficult issue in their life themselves. If you're looking for an easy solution to avoid your role or responsibility in the matter, then a spell will not work.

I am very busy writing my books, working in TV and film, looking after my coven, and helping people—but there is always a strange and wonderful synchronicity in the way magick manifests in my life, and somehow, even though it doesn't add up on paper, there is always time for everything! And the more I am in the public eye I find that, rather than demystifying my craft and diluting its essence, my personal practice is evolving to be more profoundly spiritually rewarding and also more occult and mysterious than ever. I am a very rational and primarily skeptical person, and as a solitary Witch I often needed a lot of "proof" before I was prepared to accept some of the extraordinary aspects of magick. But now that I have my coveners to share, discuss, and verify these experiences with, my life is unfolding to be even more full of magickal potential.

I have traveled the world many times over to speak about Witchcraft and met many Witches of varying levels of experience and commitment. The overwhelming impression I get is confirmed by statistical evidence that Witchcraft is the fastest-growing spiritual path in the Western world, and the religion of Witchcraft (Wicca) is one of the fastest-growing religions. The only other religion experiencing a similar explosion in popularity is Buddhism.

Information on Witchcraft's traditions is relatively new (cohesive records and teachings of its practice are, at the most, only half a century old or so). Because of this, it is relevant that modern ways of expressing what is fundamentally an ancient and innate way of experiencing and expressing our spirituality continue to mushroom. By encouraging this, we present-day Witches are forging new magickal paths even as we stay under the same magickal sky as our ancestors.

After nineteen years as a practicing Witch, I feel it is now appropriate to create a guide to meet the needs of this proliferation of "newcomers" to the Craft through the concept of a coven: to encourage individual means of expression within the Craft as well as to explain and demonstrate some basic structures that can help individuals coordinate their spiritual lives and magickal activities with others for positive results that are ultimately greater than the sum of their parts.

I have tailored this book to specifically encourage you to break out and do it your way. There are other books that generously spell out traditional coven structuring and practices, but I wanted this book to document and illustrate a more fluid and intuitive approach to covencrafting. I know there are Witches out there with the time and desire to create their own elaborately structured coven, based mostly on others' relatively fixed approaches and ideas, but there are also many others who just want to get together and make magick and enjoy and honor nature both around them and inside them in an easy yet potent way. This book responds to that perspective and is a guide to getting into Witchcraft, feeling magickal, and being together . . . now!

I hope you find this book a worthy addition to your library and that it helps guide you along your personal path of Witchcraft by illuminating a welcoming and empowered environment in which to create your very own magick with others.

So I have kept this book deliberately open and flexible. There is a lot of room for you to inject your own unique flavor into the proceedings of your coven and personal witchy development. Some may find this a blessing and think, "Great, I don't have to worry about getting lots of things wrong and remembering tons of stuff to say," but others may say, "I don't like making it up myself, I want to be told what to do." I know that coming from a Catholic upbringing, where you are encouraged to experience ritual in a very passive and receptive state, initially it can be a bit overwhelming to realize the reins of your spiritual life are in your own hands. But it's at this point that you just need to let go, trust your intuition, and let the horse steer itself. You'll always end up where you want to be.

Blessed be,

Fiona

What a Witch Is

A Witch is the woman standing next to you in line at the supermarket, the man sitting next to you at the train station, and the girl waving hello to her friends at school. Modern Witches are just that—modern; not cackling old hags brewing foul-smelling concoctions in cauldrons.

Nor are they all rotund, rosy-cheeked medieval revivalists (though some are!). Witchcraft is not a fashion statement: it's a spirit statement. However, when in L.A., you could be forgiven for sometimes thinking differently. We are doused in sunshine at least 80 percent of the year and yet I see a lot of fabulously glamorous gothic types covered in heavy black lace and satin at hot, public, witchy gatherings! Local, famous Witches like the legendary Louise Huebner (check out her classic recording "Seduction Through Witchcraft"), who was very visible through the '70s and '80s, was a mysterious seductress with her exotic, dark eyes and hair. Raven of Raven's Flight in North Hollywood is an archetypal Mother Goddess with her full figure and Arthurian garments. My good friend Lorna, owner of Silverlake's Cauldron, comes from a movie stylist background and is very gorgeous, and then there is my other good friend Jymie who owns the legendary Panpipes in Hollywood—she looks like she's come straight out of the mosh pit at a Metallica concert! We Witches are a very diverse bunch, but we respect and love each other's uniqueness and find strength in our diversity, and for all our differences, there are a few basic ideologies that we all share.

Nature Is Sacred

Modern Witches, though often living busy urban lives, find nature divinely empowered; we acknowledge and respect as sacred the spirit within all things, animate and inanimate. We consider it our duty to repair, heal, and conserve the environment and all life on this planet as constructively as we can.

I remember a particularly profound experience of the "(w)holiness" of nature over ten years ago when I was touring with my old band Def FX through the lush hinterland of northern New South Wales in Australia. After three weeks on the road, I was totally toxic—my lungs were caked with three weeks' worth of smoke from the gigs, and I felt buried in the metal cesspool on wheels that was our van speeding down the highway. My body was trapped but my gaze followed the gentle swells and jutting peaks of the surrounding mountain range, and suddenly I felt something in me shift. Instead of looking at the mountains, I became them. My muscles were heavy, damp earth; my blood was trickling streams; and my breath was the wind that spiraled in and out of the trees. I was a Lady of the Mountain and utterly present in this reality. I had a profound sense of patience and eternity and also an intense underlying sensation of *growing*—slowly but so powerfully that it was almost violent. I could feel each blade of grass jutting out of my skin; my bones became the gnarled roots of trees easing themselves in and out of the earth that was me. I was as close to knowing heaven as I'd ever been in my life at that point—a nirvanic sense of bliss, all the more for the sensation of my free, blissed-out spirit being juxtaposed with the grotty reality my physical body was in. I was overwhelmed at how utterly magnificent nature is.

I have experienced this feeling many times since when I commune with nature—the palpable sense of my physical self seeming to evaporate into bubbles of energy that then disperse into other life forms, yet still maintaining a sentient sense of self while within these forms. When I think of nature as sacred, I think from a Darwinist perspective—that as a species we evolved from this biosphere, and we are intimately connected to all life forms upon it: the stuff of oceans, mountains, stars, animals, and trees is all within us. When I consciously connect with this, I know I can align my spirit with the spirit of all living things, and after that first experience I can now make my physical sense of self "shift" to accommodate this alignment when I am doing ritual.

There Is a Goddess and a God

One of the most appealing things to many people drawn to Witchcraft in modern times is our acknowledgement of the Goddess, the feminine principle of divinity. It's not just women who find this attractive—men do too, shut off as they have been from the sensual feminine in themselves due to patriarchal dominance. Most Witches like to experience the feminine in the form of the triple-faced Goddess of the Moon: Maiden, Mother, and Crone, her presence between the worlds reflected in the waxing, full, and waning phases of the moon. I also love the image of the great Earth Mother, Gaia. My personal altar features a green statue of her sitting with a benevolent smile and huge, pregnant belly on which our blue planet is painted. The statue is called "The Millennial Gaia" and is designed by my friend Oberon Zell of Mythic Images.

The God of Witchcraft is most often venerated as the Horned Lord of the Forests, representative of the active, growing principle of life on Earth. He has many names: Pan, Cernunnos, and the Green Man are a few, and he is popularly depicted as half man, half beast—generally with a buff torso atop a hairy, cloven-hoofed pair of legs.

Witches often find inspiration in the goddesses and gods of many different cultures. We may relate to them as existing in their own right, like wise friends upon which we can call for counsel and guidance, or we may access them from a Jungian perspective as projected thoughtforms and archetypes of human social and spiritual evolution. However we choose to relate to them individually is fine. The main thing to acknowledge (in a predominantly patriarchal society) is that in addition to the widely accepted masculine principle of divinity there is the omnipresent feminine divine when you are a Witch.

Importantly, Witches do not see the God/dess as being separate from ourselves—we see them as being within us, of us, and us of them. Thus, every Witch leads themselves and can eventually be Priestess and Priest of the Craft. These titles are more a statement of experience and commitment than of superiority.

At Every End Is Another Beginning

Most Witches believe in reincarnation—that is, the soul's journey through various lives and physical forms, learning, growing, and knowing its divine purpose. My rational, scientific mind has a problem accepting this euphemistic notion of humans evolving from lesser creatures to perfect creatures.

What is "good" and "perfect" anyway? As I write this book, the war in Iraq rages on, and I think about the soldiers fighting for their country—on both sides. Most would agree that war and killing is wrong, but to the soldiers conditioned only to consider the battlefield of their current lives, the concept of war and killing is acceptable, because it will protect their countries' interests and their fellow soldiers. Who is to tell them they are wrong? They are only doing what they feel deep within their hearts is right. Wars break out in nature all the time. In my parents' back yard, I once watched an introduced lantana bush smother an indigenous boronia bush; was it wrong? No, it was an inevitable battle of two plants, with one looking for supremacy. The marking of territory is the way of all species. The cycles of death, destruction, and decay are as inevitable as birth, growth, and renewal. I do not support war by any means—I think humans evolving as a species, with the ability to comprehend our own death, means we should respect and nurture life more. When has war solved anything? We should use our highly developed brains to come up with smart, peaceful solutions, but I think that point in our collective evolution is still a ways off, unfortunately. Rather than reincarnation being a spiritual ladder to perfection, I choose to relate to it as more a process of inherited cellular genetic memory. In my genes is the DNA of my ancestors, and their lives and experiences sometimes awaken in me when I meditate or dream deeply. Essentially, my consciousness unravels their existence from the double-spiral helix within me, and I can relive their experiences as a part of me. I wrote at length about this in my first book, *Witch: A Magickal Journey*. It still amazes me that I once had recurrent regressive dream therapy that revealed to me a previous life as a Jewish child living in Northern Europe during the Second World War and who was put to death in a gas chamber. What makes this extraordinary is that when I later searched for my biological parents in my late twenties, I found that my father was Jewish, born in Hungary, and I had relatives who had been in Hitler's prisoner-of-war camps (so yes, I am a Jewitch!).

What comes after life? I don't need to know to make this life worth living—although the energy that inhabits us has to go somewhere. I really like the idea of being buried under a tree so that I nurture it and perhaps become a part of its cycle of life. The Celts used to plant sacred trees like oak, ash, and elder on people's graves, so maybe I'll ask for that in my will. But I'm pretty sure I would prefer to be cremated and have my ashes scattered at sea or thrown to the winds off the side of a mountain. I have no idea what the energy that is me will transform into—but I am interested in finding out!

Some Witches believe in Summerland, a witchy heaven that functions the same way as the Christian concept of heaven, only it's not as hard to get in!

But I don't need a promise of heaven to make this life worth living. When we die, I think what happens is that our brains still operate for a few minutes after our heart has stopped and we can ponder our death as we fade out. It is actually at this moment I think we can perhaps have some influence as to what plane of astral existence we go to. Our consciousness could act like a slingshot and project us into our next reality—but this is all conjecture. I am not in a hurry to do it, but I am certainly going to relish the experience of dying. I'm sure it will be quite extraordinary.

The Laws of Witchcraft

Do what you will, as long as you harm none: The first law is self-explanatory and clear. Do not willfully use your craft to hurt others in any way.

The Laws of Witchcraft

1: Do what you will, as long as you harm none

2: Do what you will, but do not interfere with another's will

3: As you send out so returns threefold

Do what you will, but do not interfere with another's will: The second law needs to be understood so that you do not use your magick on another person without their consent, even if it is for something as well-meaning as a healing spell. You should always wait to be asked or ask for the recipient's consent yourself if you desire to perform a spell that could affect them in any way. In some circumstances, however, it is impossible to ask for permission, and in these instances you must be prepared to accept the consequences—good or bad—if you go ahead and perform a spell.

As you send out so returns threefold: The third law is also worthy of some clarification. It does not mean "Oh, I'd better do nice things so three times' nice things come back to me" or "I'd better not do bad things in case three times' bad comes back to me." The law really means that we must be aware of and responsible for our actions. A wise Witch would never intentionally want to cause harm to another, no matter how heinous their behavior may be—she would sooner do a healing spell for the situation and perhaps in extreme cases a binding spell to prevent further harm. And a wise Witch, when doing good, always does so unconditionally, without expecting reward. As such, she is honoring the healing and nurturing aspects of her craft.

Magick Is the Art of Creating Change with Will

Witches have strong wills. I am often asked by people starting out, "How do I know I am really a Witch?" I tell them to ascertain the strength of their will. It is one skill that we must arm ourselves with to truly be credible. Developing and training our will is our greatest discipline. With a strong will, a Witch can accomplish anything. Add to that some carefully chosen crystals, herbs, incantations, and a full moon, and you have spellcasting—the magickal way to add an extra kick to the power of your will to ensure you get the results you want.

All Acts of Love and Pleasure Are Sacred to the Goddess

Sex is totally sacred. I like to have an orgasm at night, offering my bliss to the universe for positive healing and growth, or perhaps I channel it into manifesting a goal that I desire. It's much more fun than saying a prayer, and a lot more effective in encouraging change. By this, I mean I get more positive results using orgasmic energy in spellcasting than I ever did saying a prayer to God and asking for his good favors when I was young Catholic girl.

In Witchcraft we make love and offer orgasmic energy to honor the land, and our fertility rites and rituals are seen to bless and ensure continuing abundance of the earth and in our lives.

In Perfect Love and Perfect Trust

I love this saying. It is a part of my morning coven dedication: "In perfect love and perfect trust, I dedicate myself to the universal forces of magick." It is a beautiful statement of peace and harmony with all things.

With Harm to None and for the Good of All

This is said nearly always at the end of spellcasting and rituals to reaffirm the Witch's Law (also called the Wiccan Rede): "Do what you will, as long as you harm none." One of the implications of this saying is that your actions or work should always be "for the good of all." Even though "good" can be subjective, this statement serves to anchor the efforts of Witches in the positive.

During a workshop I gave at the Bodhi Tree Bookstore on Melrose—it is a Hollywood institution that has been stocking enlightened books and other products since the '70s—a young Witch, flushed and intoxicated with her newfound powers, said she wanted to help someone who needed it. "Is it okay to do a spell to help them if they don't ask me?" she asked. I replied that it wasn't. It is a bit of a conundrum, but not interfering with another's will applies to *all* areas of their life, even if you just want to do something that you think will be nice for them. In fact, the difficulty the person is experiencing could be an essential part of their personal evolution. I suggested to her it would be better to do a general spell of goodwill for all people and work on exuding a powerful healing presence herself. When the person is ready to be healed, they will most likely ask her then. I know she meant well, but she also asked how she should let people know she was a Witch because she wanted to share her empowerment with them. I told her we don't go around telling people unless they ask. One of the quickest ways to unplug yourself from the power socket of universal magick is to be self-aggrandizing. The serious weight of the Craft will bring you crashing back down in an instant.

It's All Good

As a rule, Witches celebrate all miraculous expressions of the human spirit; in other words, religions. All paths eventually want to arrive at the same place—a state of happiness, purpose, and meaning. Because Witches believe we are embodiments of the God/dess, we try to act like the best of them! We educate ourselves about different, serious mainstream, indigenous, and fringe religions of the world so that we can intelligently express respect and tolerance for them.

Coming Out of the Broom Closet

How many times has this phrase been bandied about and wryly smiled at? Yet it is still relevant despite the enormous steps forward that the Craft has enjoyed in experiencing tolerance and acceptance in general society. Unfortunately, there is still a lot of fear, negativity, and misinformation out there. In the next section, "Witchcraft: Past, Present, and Future," I explain in some detail the origins of the ridiculous accusations about Witches: that we worship Satan and are malevolent, dangerous, and committed to harming small children and animals. Now most modern Witches are well-equipped with concise and enlightened statements to nip that kind of negativity in the bud, like:

- You have to be Christian to believe the devil exists—there is no Satan to me because I am not Christian.

- The roots of my spiritual path are pre-Christian and have their source in ancient Pagan traditions of nature worshipping and animism.

One of the things I had to master when I first moved to Hollywood as an aspiring TV producer/writer/presenter was learning to love Kinko's. Everyone who comes to make it here ends up at these twenty-four-hour photocopying centers at some point, copying and collating various items of media coverage on themselves. These become the ubiquitous press packs that will hopefully attract the attention of the people you want to do business with.

In Hollywood, everyone is always on the lookout for a celebrity or a potential celebrity. So as often happens when a stranger looks over my shoulder at a magazine or book cover I am photocopying and asks loudly, "Oh, is that you?" I wince but I have to quietly answer, "Yes."

Then they generally say (even more loudly) "Witchcraft! Are you an actress? Do you play fantasy roles? Have you been on *Charmed?*" And I have to say (even more quietly) "No, Witchcraft is my spiritual path." More often than not they will reply, "Wow, that's really cool," but once someone fished around in their bag and gave me a pamphlet on Scientology and said I needed help! Scientology is very popular in Hollywood and I have some good friends who are Scientologists, but given that it has a more eccentric reputation than Witchcraft I had to laugh when this happened.

In a nutshell, here's what you can say about what a Witch is if you're ever cornered in Kinko's or confronted by any curious, or perhaps hostile, person:

"Modern Witchcraft does not have anything to do with black magic or Satanism; nor is it anti-Christian. It is a positive spiritual path (or *religion*, if you prefer) honoring the Goddess and God and one of the fastest growing in the Western world. Witchcraft encourages personal empowerment by doing rituals and spells for good and by living a responsible life that is in harmony with the environment and all living things."

Witchcraft: Past, Present, and Future

I have written about the herstory of Witchcraft at length in my first book, *Witch: A Magickal Journey*, but here is some material I haven't commented on specifically before, as well as some fresh projections on where Wicca/Witchcraft is headed in America.

Past

The origins of modern Wicca/Witchcraft are found in pre-Christian Pagan practices such as Celtic and Teutonic nature cults, the mystery traditions of ancient Greece and Rome, and later in the speculative religious science of the Gnostics and the Zoroastrians.

As Christianity gradually exerted its dominance throughout the early part of the last millennium, it declared all faiths and practices other than itself heretical and worthy of persecution. This culminated in the Inquisition in the mid- to late-1400s, and in 1484 Pope Innocent VIII issued the Witchcraft bull (an official papal document) that stepped up the Roman Catholic Church's war against so-called Witches. The bull appeared two years later as a preface to a book commissioned by the pope called the *Malleus Malificarum* (Hammer of the Witches) that was published as a guide to Witch hunting—that is, capturing and punishing anyone the pope considered a threat to the authority and power of the church. Historians disagree over the number of those tortured and killed as "Witches" over the next 400 years (the figure varies from a probable 40,000 to a very unlikely six million), but it was obviously far, far too many!

The church's concept of Witchcraft relied on encouraging superstition and hysterical fear in the hearts and minds of a gullible, oppressed public. The accusation of "Witch" became handy to those seeking to amass power and wealth, and rarely had anything to do with legitimate proof of any wrongdoing. But what kind of "legitimate proof" could there be when the charges were for holding Black Masses with the Devil himself in attendance or for turning into an animal and flying away? The charge against Witches was also a direct charge against women, because the *Malleus Malifi-carum* declared that the powers of the Witch came from "carnal lust"—and at that time this was directly attributed to female sexuality. This is ironic, considering the personal behavior of Pope Innocent VIII was quite carnal and lusty: for a start, he sired numerous children.

During this long period, Pagan ways went underground and were likely practiced in secret, but not necessarily in any cohesive, organized way. Some modern Witches believe that Wicca, the Craft of the Wise, was practiced intact over the past 400 years to enjoy a resurfacing in the mid-twentieth century, when new initiates such as Gerald Gardner and Doreen Valiente began to publicize the Craft. According to this theory, covens such as Gardner and Valiente's held the secrets of the Old Ways as they had been practiced for centuries. The more likely explanation, however, is that the post-Gardnerian version of the Craft is a reinvention, with elements of the ancient reinterpreted and restructured for new generations, much as old songs are constantly rearranged for new audiences. Either way, people like Gardner and Valiente set about reinstating the legitimacy and acceptance of the Craft by making information available about this resilient and versatile spiritual path. The Gardnerian tradition expounds ritual structure and traditions, Masonic ritual, Aleister Crowley's OTO (Ordo Templi Orientis) practices, Gnostic and Rosicrucian beliefs, and indigenous tribal shamanic practices with which he was so familiar, being a keen amateur anthropologist.

In 1951 the anti-Witchcraft laws of England were repealed, and Gardner's and Valiente's books and presence increasingly captured the public's imagination, spearheading a "revival" of the Old Ways not only in their native UK but crossing the ocean to the U.S.A. too. In the 1960s and 70s, the flamboyant Alex Sanders and his wife, Maxine, who were inspired by Gardner, forged their own tradition that was essentially similar but incorporated more traditions from Qabalah and Ceremonial Magic. Public Witches like Sybil Leek wrote exposés and appeared on television and radio, Wicca continued to grow, and the public gradually began to learn that Witches were absolutely not in league with the Devil.

The New Age explosion of the 1980s gave Witchcraft more room to be heard. Influential and politically active writers and Witches like Starhawk and Z. Budapest and charismatic individuals like Ray Buckland and Scott Cunningham made more information available and palatable for a spiritually and magickally hungry public. In some aspects of Western society, however, negative stereotypes lingered, with Witchcraft still being treated as Satanic and/or fantasy.

In the 1990s, the door to the world of Witchcraft was pushed open further again, with writers and public people like Phyllis Curott, Silver Ravenwolf, and Titania Hardie (and me) releasing books and being active in the media, thus making our presence felt at a mainstream level. At the same time the general public's interest in magick and Witchcraft exploded, stimulated by a rash of television shows like *Buffy*, *Charmed*, and *Sabrina* and movies like *The Craft*, *Practical Magic*, and the Harry Potter films.

I've already mentioned that Witchcraft is now one of the fastest-growing spiritual paths/religions in the Western world, with a strong presence in the everyday world and an even stronger one on the Internet. Recently I was watching the DVD of the 1973 classic horror movie, *The Wicker Man* (a story about a detective searching for a missing girl on a remote island who uncovers a strange cult that practices Pagan fertility rites). In the extras there was an interview with the producer, who said the movie was fraught with production and distribution difficulties that initially spelled disaster, but over time it had grown enormously in popularity and stature to become, now, a significant cult movie (so significant, in fact, that at the time of this writing, a blockbuster remake starring Nicolas Cage and directed by Neil LaBute has just been completed). The final statement the producer made was, "The thing about this movie is the more you cut it back, the more it grows." I think this can apply to Witchcraft too: the more resistance it comes up against, the more it cleverly adapts and evolves.

Present

Witchcraft and the Law: As I mentioned earlier, the anti-Witchcraft laws were repealed in England in 1951. Anti-Witchcraft laws that originated in Europe during the Burning Times were carried over into the New World of America as well. The infamous Salem Witch Trials took place in the 1690s. The "Witches" at Salem were not burned at a stake, as they had been in Europe, but were tortured to exact "confessions" and then, if the "Witches" survived, they were hanged. So extreme was the hysteria in Salem that even a dog was accused and killed for being a Witch. The anti-Witchcraft laws were mostly overturned across the country as Neopaganism and Witchcraft took root in the 1950s, flourished in the '60s and '70s, and ultimately received legal recognition as a religion (Wicca), earning legal tax exemption status for its churches. Anti-Witchcraft laws did remain in some areas of the country until 1985, when these local laws were overturned by the Supreme Court, which additionally declared discriminating against someone on the basis of their religion illegal. Even in these politically oppressive times, the U.S. military chaplain's handbook includes rites of passage for Wiccans.

One area of potential contention, however, revolves around the Witch's dagger or athame. Essentially a dual-bladed knife, an athame is never used for cutting anything solid, but it certainly can be considered a weapon by those who don't understand its ritual significance and use. As such, responsible, discreet behavior is advised when transporting and using it in public at gatherings, should you own one. I have mentioned this before, but when traveling by plane it is always worth remembering to make sure you put your athame in the bags that go in the undercarriage of the plane—these days more than ever. When I was doing talks and workshops around the country for my first book, I kept forgetting to do this. There were many times I held everyone up at the metal detector as the previously bored but now hyperactively excited security guards fished the twelve-inch blade with the mermaid handle out of my carry-on bag.

The penalties for carrying potential weaponry are much more severe now in this age of fear of terrorism, so be smart and don't wave your athame around in public unless you are engaged in a legitimate religious ritual for which you have your local council's approval.

Techno-Pagans and Eco-Wicca: The current ideology and practices of Witchcraft can be seen, to a degree, as the reemergence of indigenous spiritual practices of Northern European Pagan tribes (like the Celts), but there is also a very modern twist: we Witches embrace technology and are largely computer savvy. We actively use the Internet to learn more about our craft, share information, and connect with other like-minded souls.

Unlike our Pagan ancestors, we don't just attempt to live in harmony with the earth; we also see it as our duty to actively work to heal the damage done by years of negligent and thoughtless human trampling, and we seek to minimize further harm as much as possible. We approach our earth-based magick with a scientific slant, embracing concepts such as quantum physics to explain psychic phenomena and to refine and enhance our sacred art of spellcasting. As widely available information exposes us to the whole of human spiritual experience, our path becomes more varied and eclectic, with aspects of other nature-worshipping and polytheistic paths crossing and entwining with ours.

Conjuring a Religion: Some people have issues with the possibility of Witchcraft being "fabricated" as a fantastical and euphemistic mishmash of wishful thinking and fairy tales.

But are not all religions/spiritual paths fabricated at some point anyway? Contemporary Witchcraft may not have an unbroken connection to the most ancient traditions of European magic, as some earlier Wiccan books claimed, but this doesn't negate it any more than the Genesis-debunking discovery of Darwinian evolution stopped Christianity in its tracks. It is natural and inevitable that religions and spiritual practices will emerge reflecting the cultural, social, and spiritual evolution of our species for as long as we continue to inhabit this planet.

The idea of my interest in Witchcraft being real and credible played very much on my mind in my early witchy years. I didn't want to think that I was jumping on to some exotic trend as I dove deeper into the Craft through my late teens and early twenties. When I think back now I find it interesting that I can analyze my childhood and see how many "practices" of Witchcraft I was intuitively incorporating into my life before I had read any book on Witchcraft (or even watched *Bewitched* on TV). As a very small child I had been exposed to the image of the Good Witch of the North and the Wicked Witch of the West in *The Wizard of Oz*, but I certainly knew nothing about the Craft. However, I always experienced nature as magickal from as early on as I can remember.

I used to think I could control the wind—I would make wishes by floating leaves on the river and watching them being carried away to come true. I would leave offerings out on a flat rock on the edge of the cliff in front of our house for the flower spirits. I see these acts as being the same as the positive spells and nature-honoring rituals of my later years as an educated Witch. I did not perform these actions to harm, control, or mislead another (as the Wicked Witch of the West, or Samantha's mischievous mother Endora on *Bewitched*, did)—that never occurred to me. I did the rituals to emphasize and enjoy my feelings of connectedness with the miraculous natural world around me. I would play in the bush for hours, wandering along the tracks and trails that our neighbor's horses carved through the bush when he let them wander off (they always returned home). I would pick bush flowers like the tiny purple boronia and the starry white flannel flowers with their sage green centers like little pillows and always thank the plant and leave an offering of some sort—a feather, pretty pebble, or a kiss. I would stare at the flowers, enjoying their shape, texture, and color for so long that often a mist would form around them; perhaps it was their auras that my vision distinguished.

I would sneak out of the house and go and sit by the river, drunk with the beauty of the sunlight dancing on the water as it flushed over my toes, cold and pure. My fingers would touch the sparkles in the granite rock that I sat on, and I would feel shivers of electricity shimmer into my hands as I absorbed the energy of the ancient stone. In my later years, when I started to read books on Paganism and Witchcraft, my mind often went back to those pure, sacred moments of my childhood . . . and I realized I had been a Witch all along.

In this regard, I think there *have* been people practicing "Witchcraft" all along: experiencing a tangible connection and communication with the earth that can be interpreted in a spiritual context. At its heart, the Craft's modern-day practices beat most strongly with this fact: heaven is here on earth.

Future

Where is Witchcraft going? Wherever it is, it will bring together more voices, more diversity, and more celebration of its inclusiveness. As we become a global village and the borders between culture, society, and religion blur, the indigenous spiritual paths of our planet seem to be merging and our Craft practiced by anyone in the human genetic melting pot.

Witchcraft's unique insistence on the empowerment of the individual to be God/dess is our strength. The fact that Wicca will never be shaped or dominated by one book, one voice, or one vision is our guarantee of relevance and survival. I think Witchcraft is the smartest spiritual path on the planet in this respect. It truly is an egalitarian, positively evolved, and empowered expression of the human spirit.

Covencrafting

There are so many ways to form a coven. Most books on the subject will encourage a traditional style based on Gardnerian principles, like the excellent *Coven Craft* by Amber K. But I think as Witchcraft evolves, a more amorphous or less-structured coven "crafting" is coming into being, reflecting the modern structure of our society and the more contemporary, and less gender-specific, roles that women and men play. In this chapter, I suggest new ways of forming a coven and provide a basic skeleton of practices. Then it's up to you to fill in the rest.

Let's not forget that one of the weaknesses of the mainstream patriarchal religions is their rigid adherence to the times of old: methods and attitudes that reflect life as it was hundreds and even thousands of years ago. Wicca has a wonderful modern representation that is rooted in medieval imagery and concepts, but that is only one side of it. There are Wiccans who wouldn't be caught dead in velvet robes and surrounded by Arthurian props, preferring to be dressed in Donna Karan and circled by chic aromatherapy candles bought at Neiman Marcus!

In encouraging Wicca and Witchcraft to grow and be a vital, healthy reflection of humanity's evolving spiritual state, we need to look deeper than the surface, beyond the words and the props, to examine what the core beliefs and practices of Witchcraft are:

- Nature is a divine expression of the life force; thus, nature is empowered and sacred.

- We are nature. The human species is evolved of this biosphere, our existence co-created, co-existing and thus intricately entwined with the planet Earth and every living and non-living thing upon it.

- We are God/dess.

- Heaven is here on earth because we live here, and the greatest happiness, freedom, and peace that mainstream religions promise upon death is to be found here and right now.

Witchcraft is a way for us to live our lives as divine and empowered. It is a way of looking at and living within life. Witchcraft's tools, rituals, and ideas exist to help us connect and experience the Witches' view of the world: that is, heaven is now; every expression of love and pleasure is sacred to the God/dess; that death, destruction, and difficulty are natural and necessary in the cycle of all things; that every human is "super-naturally" empowered and can create their lives to be what they want and need.

As the popularity of Witchcraft explodes, there are more newcomers and beginners than experienced and adept Witches, and this opens up the possibility of different types of covens. Essentially a coven is a group of Witches that meets with a common purpose to learn and grow together, thus forming a community.

You may have come across "traditional" covens, which claim a reasonably long lineage of initiated Witches and insist that you are not a real Witch unless you are initiated into a coven by its high priestess and/or high priest. Obviously, though, the first coven had to start somewhere. At some point in time, the first-ever group of Witches gathered together as inexperienced as each other but with an enormous desire to learn together, grow together, and experience together.

I will not be giving guidelines in this book on how to form a traditional coven; for example, a Gardnerian, Alexandrian, or Dianic one. Generally they have pretty strict rules and methods of initiation, which are created to encourage positively disciplined theory and skill-learning, and they maintain their tradition as they feel is appropriate. In fact, some of these paths prohibit the general sharing of knowledge and methods, and have such a strict initiation process that it can only be taught by an elder of the tradition.

I have written this book more for people who have been doing their own magickal research, practicing as solitaries, and who are now keen to get together with a group of like-minded individuals to take it further. Several times over the years I have had the opportunity to be initiated into traditional covens of various paths. After an initial period of consideration I always decided not to proceed, for various different reasons, often because I would be traveling so much with my work. It just wasn't feasible to commit to a group that met regularly. And sometimes I decided that the people inviting me to join weren't really the kind of people I could commit to the traditional period of a year and a day to hang out with. Sometimes one day was enough! I have respect for traditional covens, though I don't relate to the hierarchical attitude that some have. I think anyone who is drawn to the Craft has the right to experience it, but that also means that people in a coven have the right to say no to someone who they don't think will fit in!

Finding An Established Traditional Coven

I think the best method of finding a credible and trustworthy traditional coven is to contact reputable Pagan and Wiccan alliances and groups throughout the United States. There is a suggested list of these and their details in the "Websites & Contacts" section at the end of this book. A great place to start is the wonderful online resource website for Pagans and Witches, The Witches Voice, www.witchvox.com, for their knowledge of various groups and covens operating in your area.

So what's the solution? Well, the kind of coven that is fast gaining popularity and is really what this book is about is the eclectic coven. This is a group of people who are Witches of varying levels of experience coming together with a structure based on that of a traditional coven, but without a hierarchical attitude and with a more flexible approach to practicing and evolving together.

This is what my coven is here in L.A., and it makes sense that at this moment I am the "leader," as I am the most experienced. In an eclectic coven, "leader" generally means that you are the one who calls/emails everyone to initiate the gatherings if there is a sabbat coming up or a full moon gathering to be had. You will be the one initially writing up the rituals, or finding ones to follow out of various books, and delegating various tasks for the other coveners. You may even be the one buying all the coven props too (a coven petty cash tin is a very good idea—check out the "Let's Get Going" chapter for ideas on this). In my coven, this is how things happen, but there is a lot for the other members, Tri and Zorrita, to contribute in an everyday sense. They each maintain their personal coven shrines, they each have tasks to do that I have assigned them—whether it is writing an ode to the Goddess, a wish list for the next new moon ritual, or memorizing invocations for an upcoming ritual. I might ask Tri to call Zorrita and check on her availability, or I might ask Zorrita to pick up the black agate crystals we need for a ritual.

When we started I would cast a circle, but only until the girls had sufficient experience in taking part in a circlecasting ritual. Now we share the task equally. At a point where everyone is comfortable with their "Witchcraft 101"—basically knowing how to cast a circle and developing a thorough and confident mental and emotional connection with the goings-on within a circle—then the "leading" can be shared. A couple of years after starting out on my own, I remember feeling pretty comfortable and knowledgeable in what I was doing—but now, nineteen years down the track, I can see that I have extensive knowledge, and this forms a foundation for me to be far more intuitive in my practice. Having said that, though, I love it when someone else takes charge! There is a different energy to be experienced when you are contributing to the experience rather than initiating it.

One of the things I like most about interacting with newcomers to the Craft on my website forum is that I am continually reminded, by their questions and concerns, of just how long and complex a path I have crafted for myself. I like the feeling of achievement this gives me, but it doesn't make me feel "better" or superior to anyone else, it just puts into perspective the way Witchcraft is not something you do, it's something you become—and become and become! The advice I give everyone is just to hang in there and feel free to take things slowly. If it helps to link up with other people to share the journey with, then go for it.

Following are three structures that, as I see it, can best be adapted to enhance the practices and experiences of new Witches seeking to travel with others.

The Working Group

This arrangement is practical for a group of relative "newbies" and is a precursor to a formal coven further down the track. Rather than practicing formal circlecastings and full moon gatherings, this is more like a study group. You get together once a week or more to talk about Witchcraft, to read together and share personal experiences. A good way to kick-start a working group is to choose a book to read. Everyone could read a few chapters a week, make some personal notes, and then get together to discuss it. You may start to write your group's impressions and thoughts in another book, and this could evolve to be a Book of Shadows if you do eventually take the plunge and create a coven together.

A working group, when persevered with, does usually result in a coven, either eclectic or teen, or the members may then feel drawn to seek membership in an established traditional coven.

The Eclectic Coven

This is a more formal coven structure and is formed around a minimum of one very adept (experienced) Witch, who acts as guide and leader for a group of other committed new Witches. This coven meets on auspicious occasions like the full moon (esbats) and sabbats, as well as an initial weekly meeting to get a strong covenworld started.

Something else an eclectic coven will likely need to do (and a teen coven—see the next section) is a formal education course for all members so that everyone is educated on the principles and practices of Witchcraft. This is a "Witchcraft 101" course, so to speak, which I've mentioned before.

A "covenworld"

is the astral projection of the union of the coven members' personal energies and intentions. A coven-world exists "between the worlds" at all times, not just in the physical world when the members are gathered together. It needs to be built strongly, like a house, with repeated reaffirmations of its existence until it is powerful, resilient, and available to all coven members as a spiritual retreat and recharging hotspot.

This is similar to the various "year and a day" initiation degrees of traditional covens. It is like going to night school for a while, and it is necessary. The "Witchcraft 101" chapter in this book is a helpful guide to an eclectic coven's study process. As I mention in that chapter, I highly recommend the online "Witchcraft 101" curriculums. I designed the one in this book as an eight-week course for the practical aspect, but of course the experience that is required to be a really powerful Witch is ongoing and never stops. However, you can learn the basics and build from there with one of these courses. An eclectic coven can last for years, growing and evolving, or the members can be compelled to end it sooner if things don't go as smoothly as everyone hopes. But I do think it is appropriate to commit to a year and a day, no matter what. Obstacles should be viewed as opportunities for growth, learning, and personal development. Perseverance and tolerance are essential in eclectic covens (or any coven, for that matter).

The Teen Coven

Teen Witches can be quite adept in the practical knowledge of the Craft, as I have discovered after meeting many of them in my travels! Having said that, teen coven structures and activities need to acknowledge youth and limited life experience. In teen covens, tempers tend to flare a bit more; there are more personal issues, more power struggles, and more insecurities to be confronted and dealt with. This has really only to do with the fact that no matter how wise and "old" a teenager feels (I remember feeling so old at nineteen), the reality is that you are still at the very beginning of your life's journey. Though there are certainly some teens who are more mature than others, generally teens are still finding their way, and there is a bit of territorial marking and shuffling to be done. (Adult covens have almost the same likelihood of power struggles, arguments, and perhaps even more sexual tension!)

In a teen coven, I think it is important to avoid a hierarchical structure and have leadership roles shared equally. You are all likely to have a similar degree of knowledge, and though some teens may take to Witchcraft like a duck to water, others may have to struggle with it, and a tolerant and compassionate attitude is essential. Even if someone is more experienced, there should be no high priestesses or high priests. You can all be priestesses and priests together, though I think these terms, as romantically appealing as they are, are a bit outdated. Witches are what we are and there doesn't need to be a grandiose title for coven members to know and acknowledge someone's wisdom and learning. Witchcraft's great and unique strength is unity in diversity.

Girl Coven, Boy Coven, Girl-Boy Coven, Gay Coven, Gay-Hetero Coven

In my experience, same-sex covens are generally the easiest to work with. The exception perhaps to this is a mixed-sex coven but where members are hetero female with gay male members. An all-male coven with female lesbian members is less likely to be successfully free of sexual tension, as men tend to have a different attitude toward their sexuality. By this I mean that men are more likely to be sexually distracted by a lesbian coven member than female members are by a gay male coven member. Witchcraft considers sex as sacred, and in some traditional covens sex magick is conducted by higher-degree initiates. No, I don't mean orgies, but sexual intercourse may be performed in the presence of other coven members as a means of honoring the Goddess and God made manifest in humans. Sex can also be used to raise power through orgasm for spellcasting and ritual work.

Sexual energies and tensions can be a wonderful and enriching part of a coven, but they can also be the cause of relationships breaking down in an unpleasant and nonconstructive way. Witchcraft does have an open, egalitarian attitude toward sexuality, but people are people! The analogy I can relate most to this is being in a band. When I was in Def FX in my twenties, I was the only female member in a band with three boys. During the lineup changes over seven years, I ended up dating two of them at different times—a *very* bad choice—though when you are doing something passionate and creative together like making music (and making magick), eventually hormones will boil and bubble and some sexual chemistry will result. So, especially if it is during a coven's early days, try to keep it all really simple and avoid intimate personal relationships so that you can build a strong coven foundation. Perhaps further down the track you could introduce a mixed-gender situation.

Think of your coven like a family and that it is "inbreeding" to date a coven member! In some traditional covens, like the Gardnerian tradition, it is preferable for a male and female couple to be initiated into the coven together and for them to be married or at least sexual partners. It is felt they contribute more to the power of the group by representing, and therefore honoring, the powers of procreation and nature.

But for eclectic covens and especially teen covens it may be best to avoid this. In my own coven with Tri and Zorrita, I don't actually have personal friendships with them. We just have magickal relationships, and this keeps our focus on the spiritual and magickal development in our covenworld, which we can then individually take out into the everyday world.

It may be fun to organize coven gatherings where different covens come together for socializing and perhaps romancing—sort of like a "gathering of the tribes." In one of my favorite fiction books, the now-classic *Clan of the Cave Bear* by Jean M. Auel, there is a gathering of the tribes like this every summer for the express purpose of mixing up the blood. It's very healthy and essential to the survival of the species! At this point, I would like to say that if you are really keen on having your boyfriend, girlfriend, wife, or partner in your coven, it may be better to create a working group instead. This is so you can gather and learn together in a relaxed environment without personal politics becoming involved.

When you create a coven, it's like you are creating a community—a world within (or between) worlds. The group mind that you create when the coven gets together takes on a reality of its own on the astral planes (for want of a better term). You think and act it into creation, and if you keep it charged it will be there for you to access whenever you need it. The relationship with your coveners is, by its nature, unique. Personally, I couldn't be in a coven with my closest friends in my everyday world. I have my regular friends and then I have my coven sisters. We get along fantastically, but we don't socialize in the regular sense with each other. Now, I know a lot of covens in which the members are close friends in the everyday and the eternal planes, but I find that too much of the everyday can get distracting and coven meetings become gossip sessions, not magickal meetings. Of course, after a meeting Tri, Zorrita, and I will chat, drink, and eat together to ground our energies, but we tend to talk only of esoteric subjects. We also have an agreement that there is to be nothing personal discussed before we enter the circle . . . in fact, then we don't say much at all. We approach the whole event with great seriousness and reverence. But that is just us; if we're at group gatherings like Pagan festivals we tend to loosen up a bit!

There is no easy answer—it really just comes down to personal preference about the kind of coven you form or join, but by being aware of potential pitfalls you can perhaps spot them coming and avoid them or deal with them more effectively.

Now you may have an idea of whether it would be best to start with a working group or plunge into forming an eclectic or teen coven. In any case, congratulations! Your journey is just beginning and there is a lot to do and see . . .

Bring It On

This chapter covers a range of things that need to be addressed now that you have decided you want to be part of a coven. First, how do you meet the right people? Then, when you have, what should the goals and ethics of the coven be? Is a patron God/dess necessary or just a nice idea? What should the name of the coven be if it's new? Should you take a magickal name now that you are a member of a coven? And where should you have your first meeting?

Hello—Is It Me You're Looking For?

Finding other members for your own coven can be easy or extremely hard, and looking to join an existing coven can be harder still. So where do you start? Should you directly approach people? Whether you want to establish a coven or join a coven, it is best to exercise the Witches' Creed, also called the Witches' Pyramid. *Know* what you desire to do (create or join a coven), *Will* it into being (mentally manifest the reality you desire), *Dare* to believe it will be (let the universe play its hand in making it happen), and—probably the most important and yet confounding part—*Be Silent.* As I've mentioned, Witches do not preach and we do not seek converts. "How the heck do I find people

The Witches' Pyramid

To Know

To Will

To Dare

To Be Silent

then?" you are probably asking. "And, for that matter, how many am I looking for?" A minimum of two, other than you, and up to a maximum of thirteen is generally a good rule of thumb. Remember, though, smaller covens generally run a lot more smoothly, especially when you are new to it.

I will describe something that happened in my life to illustrate what I mean when I say "Be Silent." Here in L.A., I was invited to a party by a friend who was a friend of actor Crispin Glover. I was told it would be a private affair and that there would likely be a few notable people from the occult scene, as Crispin is interested in matters to do with the unusual and unexplained. At the party I was introduced to Crispin, who was very charming and offered my friend and me some food and drink. I was sitting on an antique couch chatting with my friend when a cavalcade of stars began to arrive. Cameron Diaz, Kate Hudson, and Drew Barrymore walked in and plonked themselves down next to me. Across the room were Nicolas Cage and Lisa-Marie Presley (literally the day before they announced their divorce, though they looked perfectly happy on this night). Harry Dean Stanton and the whole main cast (except for Naomi Watts) of David Lynch's film *Mulholland Drive* (a fave of mine) were also milling around. It was turning into a surreal night, not only for the dazzling array of A-list celebrities, but for Crispin's home itself. It's a topsy-turvy Spanish castle in an artistic suburb, with doorways halfway up the wall, staircases leading nowhere, and giant beds covered in red velvet canopies. Cameron, Kate, and Drew were drinking chalices of a glowing green cocktail while Nicolas was wandering around with Lisa on his arm calling out, "Crispin! Where's Crispin?" Meanwhile, the host was on the roof with a couple of *Mulholland Drive* stars talking about the film he had just produced in which the whole cast was Downs Syndrome actors. I was enjoying my intense conversation with a gentleman named Brian, one of the notable "occult" people there. He owns Feral House Publishing and releases books by the infamous Satanist (now deceased) Anton La Vey.

The point of me describing this scenario to you is to illustrate what I mean by keeping silent. I knew that I could probably have eased myself into conversations with these various uber-celebs and dropped the words "I'm a Witch." I'm sure they would have been interested and I probably would have been invited around to Cameron's house to hold a spellcasting party. But I didn't. Engaging these people's interest would have most likely given my career here a big boost ("who you know" means a lot in this town); however, using Witchcraft as a means of self-promotion is ultimately disempowering and, to be honest, just not dignified. So I kept my mouth shut. I thought to myself, "Let them come to me." If Kate Hudson one day approaches me and says, "Fiona, I've seen your book and I'm really intrigued," or Drew Barrymore says, "I saw you on a television show, I'd like to know more," then I will happily chat about my craft.

You might think this "keep silent" approach is contradictory when I write books on Witchcraft and appear on television shows talking about the Craft, but it isn't. Readers have the choice to pick up my books and read them, and I am invited onto the television shows. Viewers can decide to watch my show or not. When I am introduced to people for the first time, I never say "Hi, I'm Fiona and I'm a Witch." In this town, where everyone is obsessed with what you "do," an introductory conversation with me generally goes like this:

"Are you a model? Are you an actress?"

"No, I'm a writer."

"Oh, what do you write?"

"Books and television shows."

"What about?"

"Witchcraft."

Just for fun, I'll tell you about another common exchange (this one usually happens if I'm conversing with a guy who is hitting on me in the patronizing and gratuitous way that is the Hollywood standard and I want to put a stop to it):

"Are you a model? Are you an actress?"

"No, I work in a bagel store."

"Oh, really . . . well, you have *great* arms, you must work out."

"No, it's from kneading all the dough for the bagels."

This generally gets a blank look—and the guy will look over my shoulder for greener pastures and wander off.

But getting back to the point of being silent—when you are looking for coven members, you must let them come to you. You can sit in your school's common room and read a book about Witchcraft and maybe someone will come up and ask what you are reading. You can put up a notice on a message board, in the physical world and/or on the Internet, saying something like, "Person interested in Wicca and Witchcraft seeking others with similar interest who live in the area of _____." (You want them to be in a close geographical location.) Don't leave your phone number—instead you could get a post office box and invite people to send their names and details there. You could make your "advertisement" more specific and say something like, "Female seeking other females to explore and develop personal and group practices of Wicca and Witchcraft. Must be serious and prepared to meet regularly."

Again, keep it discreet and do not impose yourself on others. Let them come to you—let the universe wield its "hand of fate"—then the exchange of energies between you and the people you connect with will be far more pure and powerful, with ultimately more potential.

It's the same for an online coven: don't go around emailing people that you are a Witch and want to form or join a coven. Instead post your intentions on a message board or forum and wait for people to come to you. I personally think an online coven is a little bit dry if you haven't had an "in the flesh" experience. There is something quite profound when people personally gather together that even the most passionate cyberspace coven can't quite replicate. I would strongly suggest working with people in the flesh first and maybe then having an additional cyberspace presence. For example, if one or some of you are traveling frequently, the Internet is wonderful to stay in touch and when you're all not in the same space you can do online coven gatherings rather than skipping them altogether.

One of the best ways to attract other like-minded people who are going to resonate harmoniously with you is to do a little something to "put it out there."

Spell for Attracting Coven Members

You will need:

+ One large piece of paper
+ Colored pencils in the rainbow spectrum: red, orange, yellow, green, blue, indigo, and violet
+ Salt

An object for each element:

+ Air/east: incense
+ Earth/north in the Northern Hemisphere, south in the Southern Hemisphere: crystal
+ Water/west: bowl of water
+ Fire/south in the Northern Hemisphere, north in the Southern Hemisphere: candle

Sprinkle salt in a circle that is large enough for you to sit within. Place the elemental objects in the quarters they are aligned with (i.e., north, south, east, and west) and the paper and pencils in the center (you may like to include a small table to lean on).

Take a few deep breaths and connect with the fact that you are in a sacred, empowered space. Using the red pencil, draw a circle in the center of the paper and then divide the circle into seven sections. Slowly start coloring in each section with a different color of the rainbow. This represents the harmonious diversity you seek for your coven. As you color, chant:

Colors work your perfect power
Draw to me my perfect coven.

Color the circle methodically and neatly, being careful not to go over the lines with each color. When the circle is fully colored, lick the tip of your index finger, place it in the center of the paper, and forcefully say:

I call those who are meant to be
Come from the shadows unto me
Me and I now becomes we
My coveners be here with me.

Stay for a moment in this space; you may have visions of people appear in your mind's eye. Make a note of details— perhaps hair or eye color, whatever you can pick up. Remember these so that you can recognize these kindred spirits when they cross your path.

To end the ritual, roll up the paper and place on your personal altar in the quarter of earth with a crystal on top to anchor your visualization in reality. Sweep up the salt and put it in the garbage, throwing a little over your left shoulder as you do this. Witches are not superstitious but we do honor tradition—and if you spill salt you *always* throw a pinch over your left shoulder!

Ego and the Craft

Ego gets in the way of power. People who go about big-noting themselves and their craft in a self-aggrandizing way are not true Witches. True Witches don't need to prove anything to anyone other than themselves.

Knowing When People Are Cool

One of the most common questions I hear is about finding the right people to work magick with. Ego battles, insecurities, and laziness are all problems, but more often than not I find that people who are drawn to the Craft are prepared to work on addressing those problems within themselves with positive results. Certainly part of being in a coven can include ironing out those kinks in yourself.

I am often so impressed when I visit the forum on my website and see everyone encouraging each other to be tolerant and respectful even when there is a difference of opinion, in fact *especially* when there is a difference of opinion. A common problem is that while everyone may seem hunky-dory at first, problems can arise as time goes on, and I address this specifically in the chapter "Room for Improvement." However, right now I can say there are some basic methods of screening both people coming to you and those to whom you are attracted to narrow down any potential problems.

Sun/Star Sign Compatibility

It's worth noting people's sun/star signs and ascertaining the likelihood of unproductive friction. It may not seem appropriate to bar people because of their astrological makeup, and of course there are so many varying factors that color a person, like rising signs and what planet is in what, etc. (I am not going to attempt all the variables here, but an excellent book to consult is Linda Goodman's *Sun Signs* [Harper Perennial]—it's an absolute classic.) But if you have an awareness of people's astrological profiles, then you can be forewarned of potential problems, more tolerant and solution-oriented when they occur, and also maximize the benefits of compatible sun/star sign combinations.

Gender

I mentioned in the previous chapter that same-sex covens generally run more smoothly because sexual tension is less likely to be a distraction. Often the sensual nature of Witchcraft rituals can act like an aphrodisiac that encourages certain individuals to be distracted from the task at hand. But often that's the whole point! As well as being sacred, Witchcraft is a sexy spiritual path: all acts of love and pleasure are sacred to the Goddess. This is even applicable to younger groups, though I think same-sex groupings are advisable so everyone can concentrate on their personal development and magick and throw overt female/male polarities into the mix a bit further down the track.

Deciding on Coven Ethics and Responsibilities

Coven ethics and responsibilities should be decided on and written up in the coven's Book of Shadows before the first gathering. A suggested list would be:

1. Honor personal commitments to the coven. Once you have committed to being in your coven, stand by that commitment for the agreed time (usually a year and a day). Don't flake out and be late for or miss meetings. Do the tasks that are necessary to initiate, develop, and maintain the coven. Respect the personal commitment each member has made with their effort and time by being consistent in your attitude and the application of your own efforts.

2. Keep the coven sacred by not bringing personal dramas to gatherings. (A coven meets "between the worlds," and this should be an oasis from the trials and tribulations of everyday life.)

3. Commit to creating a strong group mind. Do coven dedications/meditations every day and practice personal lifestyle choices that support the goals of the coven.

Note: There should be signed statements of intent in your coven's Book of Shadows where every new member copies the agreed list of ethics and responsibilities and signs to confirm their respect and acknowledgement of the depth of their commitment.

Choosing Your Patron God/dess

This is worth doing, as it is fun and inspirational to choose a patron god/dess for your coven. It is not essential, but most covens and groups I know have a goddess and/or god from a particular period of society and culture that best expresses the personality of their coven. My coven's patron goddess is Lilith—the first feminist—which is very appropriate for a strong, all-female coven!

I also suggest that if one of the many pantheons of goddesses and gods from different cultures and societies doesn't adequately fulfill what you want your goddess and god to be, then why not create your own?

Create Your Own God/dess

+ Write a list of the qualities you want your deity to have. Is it a god/dess of warrior spirit, of love, of intellect? Maiden, Mother, or Crone? Youth, man, wise man? An animal, human, or even alien form?

+ Create a story or myth about the origins of your god/dess and find images that depict its environment and appearance.

+ Choose a name for your deity.

+ As a group, meditate on your deity to "conjure" it into being. Based on its attributes, make regular, appropriate offerings to it. For example, if it's a goddess who emerges from the sea, make offerings of seashells and salt. The more meditation that you channel into its "existence," the more of a presence it will itself manifest and the more independence it will enjoy, enabling it to be outside of your imaginings and then become a helpful, independent entity for your coven.

It may seem strange, or even sacrilegious, to be suggesting that you create your own god/dess. However, my opinion is that all god/desses are archetypes and forms of projected

Coven Goals

To create a nurturing and stimulating environment in which to study and practice Wicca/Witchcraft together.

To honor each coven member as a sister/brother in magick and support their individual and the coven's collective aspirations.

To honor the God/dess within and without.

To help, heal, and empower people inside the coven.

To help, heal, and empower people outside the coven.

To take action to heal, protect and conserve all life on the planet.

To dispel the negative stereotypes and misinformation that exist in general society about Witchcraft.

thought, consciousness, and ideas that have evolved throughout human existence. Their qualities and appearances mirror the era and lifestyle in which they came into being. For example, modern god/desses could be considered to be John Lennon, Ghandi, and, more recently, Oprah and Anthony Robbins—religions of sorts have evolved around these larger-than-life people so that people now venerate and worship them. It's worth remembering the real role of the God/dess is actually to serve us, to teach us about ourselves and awaken us to the divinity within.

If you accept the concept of the collective unconscious, then you will probably think there is validity in acknowledging and tapping into projected thoughtforms that others have acknowledged for eons. There is strength in this if you choose to explore and have a relationship with the divine in this way. If this doesn't make sense, I'm talking about worshipping the old goddesses and gods! Or you may have a different opinion and firmly believe that the gods and goddesses actually exist, have always existed, and will continue to exist after the human life form has become extinct—which is perfectly fine! A good way to learn about deities of various cultures is to type "gods and goddesses" into your favorite Internet search engine and look at the myriad of sites that come up.

Naming Your Coven

You may like to name your coven after your patron god/dess, which is what we did for our Dark Light of Lilith coven. Or you may like to name it after a flower or fruit—for example, Eldergrove Coven held the first coven gathering I ever attended and was named after a tree sacred to the Celts. Crystals and mythical animals are popular, like "The Coven of the Emerald Dragon" (actually that sounds more like a Bruce Lee film!). But be inventive and choose a name that excites, inspires, and best expresses the essence of the coven.

Choosing Your Personal Magickal Name

Generally, magickal names are bestowed upon coven members at their initiation, but it's worth having a think about it beforehand. I did not take on a magickal name, nor did my coveners—we decided our current names are magickal enough! It's entirely up to you as to what you choose, but you may like to check the numerology of your newly acquired name to make sure that it will be aligned positively to your magickal goals. Visit www.2numerology.com for help. This Internet site is very inspirational.

Deciding Where to Gather Together

How do you get around the unfortunate negative stereotypes that exist about Witches and Witchcraft, especially when it affects deciding the best and safest venues for your gatherings? One Witch usually doesn't attract much attention, but a group of them is another thing entirely.

In my chapter on dedicating your coven, I talk about how finding a place to gather can be a challenge. One of my goals is to one day open Wiccan and Pagan Spiritual Sanctuaries—parklands and retreats where Witches and Pagans can gather to do their rituals without fear of harassment. People of all spiritual paths will be welcomed, but it will really be tailored for Witches and Pagans, with circle groves and natural altars and an eco-education center encouraging the healing of our planet. Entry and bookings (for the groves) will be by donations, which will be used to maintain the reserves.

Good places to consider for gatherings are:

+ Someone's private back yard.

+ A large living room or private balcony.

+ A community hall that can be rented out.

+ School grounds on the weekend. You may be able to organize permission from your local school to have your gathering in a private part of the grounds (though unfortunately in some parts of North America teens are being expelled from school for wearing pentagrams and declaring that they practice Witchcraft and Wicca).

+ There are Pagan-friendly retreats and camping grounds in the U.S.A. Visit websites like The Witches' Voice (www.witchvox.com) for advice on locations and also upcoming public, Pagan events.

Not-so-good places for gatherings are:

- Public parks during the day, unless you have permission from the local council. Recently I was a speaker at the Annual Pagan Day Festival held at the public Hollywood Park. It was a fantastic day, really well-organized by Jymie and Vicky of Panpipes, Hollywood, with full approval from the city council. We had curious onlookers but the crowd was predominantly Pagan and it was a peaceful and magickal day. It's a different matter, though, if your coven just rocks up to a park and starts setting up an altar. You won't be able to concentrate for the curious stares and possibly unpleasant comments you will receive, so don't even bother. Witchcraft is not about putting on a show and freaking out non-Witches. If you want to gather in a public place, go through the proper channels and get permission so that you aren't carted off by the police after some well-meaning passer-by complains that someone is waving a knife around in the park.

- Parks and beaches at night, when you think every potentially disruptive person is at home in bed. This is simply too dangerous—even the most potent circle of pure protection may not be guaranteed to keep psychos, or just plain idiots, at bay.

- A vacant property—you could be arrested for trespassing.

Be creative and you will find a safe space. Like I describe in the chapter "Dedicate Your Coven," my first gathering was on the roof of a girlfriend's house! Which actually brings up a good point, one I have made before, but it's worth repeating: if you are planning to have a midnight gathering, scope the area out during the day first. Don't just drive to a remote location and set up a circle, run around to raise power just outside the circle of firelight, and fall off the side of a cliff! This can truly happen and it is not cool! So do your preparation and familiarize yourself with the location before you gather there. If I had not been aware of the slope of a certain part of the roof just outside the circle of tealight candles we had set up, I may well have slid off into the swimming pool!

Remember, in Witchcraft the rule of thumb is to act practically as well as magickally!

Let's Get Going

You have completed the first essential step, and you have interested, committed potential coven members lined up. You even have a location secured to gather and start doing magick together; what else should you organize before you begin? Well, it's important to agree on some basic tools of Witchcraft that each of you will have. However, as I have said in all my books on Witchcraft, it's unnecessary to go out and spend a ton of money on elaborate props. A few well-selected or well-crafted (if you choose to make them yourself) tools will definitely assist you in practicing your craft. A good idea, prior to an official dedication of a coven, is for the prospective coven members to meet up and bring all their individual tools. Some people might bring a truckload, others may have nothing. In my coven I have the most extensive collection of Craft tools, only because I've been practicing the longest and I have had the most time to accumulate stuff!

People may be in different financial situations and be concerned about having to buy a lot of things (especially members of teen covens), but again I emphasize that having the most expensive, elaborate athame does not necessarily make you a superior Witch to someone who uses their pointed index finger!

Here are some basic items that Witches accumulate as they develop in the Craft. You will know if you have read various books that there are many different ritual tools and witchy items available. The lists below cover anything you would need to perform any of the rituals and spells in this book. But of course, feel free to extend your stash beyond what I have suggested below as per your personal taste and requirements!

A Witch's Personal Tool Stash

Athame: For casting a circle and channeling energy (the athame represents male energy and the fire element).

Pentacle: A brass, clay, or ceramic disc carved with a pentagram to rest your athame on or to use as a plate (it represents the earth element). For my pentacle, I use a large, flat, mother-of-pearl shell with five embedded pearls in it that I interpret as being aligned to the five points of the pentagram.

Chalice: For libations and toasting (it represents female energy).

Incense: For the air element.

Bowl: For the water element. I keep seashells in my bowl when there is no water in it, to remind me of the ocean.

Candles: For the fire element.

Individual Book of Shadows: For your personal recordkeeping.

And some extras:

Small cauldron: Good for burning petitions in (small pieces of paper with your wishes written on them; as they burn, the smoke travels your dreams to the stars).

Wand: For conjuring. Different from the athame, though some use them interchangeably. The wand is aligned with the element of air.

Mortar and pestle: For blending incenses and powders.

The next thing you should discuss is the coven stash of tools and magickal goods, which will be a little bit more elaborate. If you don't have a permanent location set up for coven gatherings, like a private room, then generally the coven goods will be kept by the "leader" of the coven and perhaps circulated among members as is appropriate. For example, I generally keep our coven totem—a wolf heart (or "Heart de Lobos" as Zorrita calls it)—on my coven shrine, along with the coven Book of Shadows. One night, however, when it was a full moon and we weren't gathering together, Zorrita took it home to place on her windowsill to capture the full moon rays so that the heart of our coven would be empowered on this night. (At the time, my apartment unfortunately didn't get direct moonlight!)

If your coven becomes large and a very professionally run outfit, you may have quite an elaborate arrangement of people contributing money and a weekly shopping list being filled so that you almost have a small store of occult supplies at your fingertips. We are pretty relaxed in our coven, though—if we need anything specific, we just organize it before the gathering and split the expenses if they amount to anything much. At the end of this chapter I have put together some tips for organizing finances and accounting, if you feel that it is appropriate to have a little coven petty cash fund going.

Witch Tip

I have a small chest at home that has various colored and shaped candles, incenses, herbs, crystals, shells, feathers, lodestones, powders, talismans, cloth bags, tarot cards (three decks), and other bits and pieces. I can always rummage through my chest and rustle up a spell or a few things required for a gathering.

The Coven Stash

Book of Shadows.

Statue of patron god/dess: (optional).

Coven candle: Only lit at coven gatherings.

Coven totem: An item of power that has special significance to the coven and represents its unity.

Chimes or bells: For ringing in the quarters (optional).

Large cauldron: For burning petitions.

Incense thurible or burner: It's a good idea to have a large incense burner for coven gatherings so that if you need to purify large spaces, objects, or a group of people, you can generate plenty of smoke!

Altar cloth: A large piece of fabric that can be spread over any surface to make it appropriate as an altar.

A general supply of different colored candles, incense blends, etc.

Books: For research and reference.

It's fun to go shopping for coven supplies! Do some research and phone ahead, though, so that you are guaranteed some success in finding the various (and sometimes obscure) items you may need. Doing this in a group is a great way to bond and for everyone to have a good comprehension of the uses of various items. If you live in an area that has absolutely no esoteric/New Age supply store, then you could surf the Internet and order things online and have them delivered to your door. At my website there are extensive lists of international suppliers (see the "Fiona Recommends" link), and also see the "Websites & Contacts" section in this book for recommended sites. It's almost like having my very own Hedwig leaving magickal surprises at my door when I shop on the 'net!

Other than shopping, you may find it appropriate to actually make some of your personal and coven tools. This may involve attending a workshop together or just sitting yourselves down and getting creative. The more grassroots interaction you have, the stronger your coven bond will be and the more effective and rewarding your activities will be together.

Can Someone Else Touch My Athame?

It's generally considered good manners to not pick up someone else's personal magickal stash. Through repeated use, certain objects like athames and wands can take on the energy of their owner and become specifically aligned to them. In theory, someone else picking them up and not respecting the significance of this magickal bond could interfere with it and the object's effectiveness in completing its magickal task. So in other words, always ask the owner if it's okay to pick something up, in case, perhaps, you need to move it to make room on the altar for the cauldron or another tool. However, shared coven tools are different, and I think it's actually really good for everyone to handle them, as they will be imbued with everyone's energy.

Personal Altar

Here's what you need:

A candle for fire: Place in the southern quarter of your altar if you are in the Northern Hemisphere (and in the northern quarter if you are in the Southern Hemisphere).

A crystal for earth: Place in the northern quarter if you are in the Northern Hemisphere (and in the southern quarter if you are in the Southern Hemisphere).

Your pentacle with your athame on top of it: Usually placed in the center.

Incense for air: Place in the eastern quarter.

The Coven Library

Personally I have over 200 books on Witchcraft and related topics. Between you and your coven members there may be a significant amount of books, and you might think it appropriate to combine all your books and form a library, or even chip in funds to purchase books specifically for a coven library. If you do this, make sure you keep a written record of the name of each book, the date of lending, and the name of the person borrowing to keep track of them. A nice idea, too, is to stick a bookplate inside the front cover so that everyone who reads and uses the book can write their name and a comment on how helpful they found the book.

Bowl for water: Place this bowl full of water in the western quarter.

Chalice: Place in the center or anywhere there is space.

An image of the Goddess and God: (optional).

An altar cloth: To denote the sacred space upon which everything is placed.

Personal Coven Shrines

In addition to your personal solitary altar, when you become a member of a coven it is a good idea to have a coven shrine featuring objects specifically related to your coven and patron god/dess. In my coven, we chose a few basic items that we agreed were appropriate to each have before adding our own personal touches. You may even feature photos of your fellow coveners. Depending on your level of experience, you may just have a coven shrine to start with and then gradually build your personal altar. As your knowledge increases and your personal practices expand to reflect this, you can stock up on your personal tools. A coven shrine makes a strong statement, both visually and magickally, that you are committed to your new community, and it can also act as a physical key or portal to your covenworld. You will be meditating and performing your morning dedication at your coven shrine, and the energy that you channel and project as you do these powerful psychic activities will attach itself to your shrine objects and empower them. Your shrine will then charge you up with the combined energies of your coven, even when you are not physically in its space.

Book of Shadows

This is a record of magickal workings and methods. You can have a personal Book of Shadows and there is also a coven Book of Shadows. In my coven, I am in charge of maintaining our coven Book of Shadows—I tend to write most of the rituals. I type them up, print them out, and then paste them in. What I also do is then email Tri and Zorrita the rituals, and they paste them in their individual

Books of Shadows with their own additional notes. If I find a cool picture of our patron goddess I will paste that in too. We have also marked it with our blood to make it ours. (See a full description of this in the "Dedicate Your Coven" chapter.)

Coven Clothing

Witchcraft is not a fashion statement, so no pointy hats and dark cloaks are required at coven gatherings! Having said that, if you want to wear these "traditional" accoutrements, feel free. However, some of the best advice I ever got from Hawthorn, the high priestess of Eldergrove coven, was: "Don't wear your cloaks into circle—they fall and drape all over the place, knocking over candles, sweeping items off the altar, and are generally very hazardous!"

Too true! You may have a romantic vision of your coven gathering together in matching dramatic black robes, with long, flowing lace sleeves and capes flung back to reveal luscious purple lining. But once you've knocked over a few candles, got covered in wax, and had people stepping on your hem and ripping it as you run around raising power, you realize that more often than not simple clothing in circle is best. I attended an open circle of the Eldergrove coven many years ago, and everyone had basic black robes with slim long sleeves over which they wore black capes, which were removed before entering the circle.

It's likely that different members will have different financial circumstances, so it's respectful to not have expensive clothing as a requirement. When my coven gathers, we usually wear slightly dressy attire in black unless it is a specific sabbat like Imbolc when we wear white or Beltane where we wear red, pink, or other luscious, fertile colors. We don our witchy jewelry: I wear my mother-of-pearl pentacle, Tri wears an obsidian double terminator wand set in silver at her throat, and Zorrita wears Mexican beads. We usually have bare feet. For our coven initiation, we got all dressed up with lots of makeup—the works! Generally, though, I wear little or no makeup and always have a shower before the gathering to wash off the accumulated energy of the day.

Do We Have to Be Naked?

Absolutely not, though you absolutely can be if you like. The only time I am ever naked in a group is at women-only gatherings. Women of varying ages and backgrounds spending the weekend together in ritual and doing workshops and at times being unified together in an utterly natural skyclad (naked) state is supremely beautiful and empowering. The purpose of being skyclad is to liberate us from our preconceived notions of class and culture and to celebrate the extraordinary human form in all its expressions. If being skyclad makes you feel uncomfortable, then do not do it.

Magickal Jewelry

In traditional groups like Gardnerian and Alexandrian covens, it is usual for women to have a large silver bangle or ring and for men to have a brass or copper bangle or ring signifying their coven membership. As a group I think it is a good idea to agree on a piece of jewelry that you each wear (as you would a wedding ring), and these can be consecrated (passed through incense smoke) and ceremonially put on during the coven dedication ceremony. You may decide to have matching pentacle necklaces, matching onyx rings, or carved silver bracelets.

Finances and Accounting

My coven operates very simply when it comes to money: as there are only three of us, it's easy to chip in and share expenses, or for one of us to say, "I'll get the candles if you can pick up juice and carrot cake for afterwards."

If I hold a Goddess Gathering, it's generally a potluck affair with everyone bringing a plate of food and a bottle of drink, and each person bringing their own candle or flowers or whatever is required for the ritual. I bring my Craft tools, cauldron, and perhaps specially blended incense. I was happy to buy our Book of Shadows and patron goddess statue as, at the time we needed them, I was a bit more cashed up than Tri and Zorrita. However, if there is a large group of you, it may be worth considering having a coven petty cash fund where everyone puts in $10 or so each meeting, and the money is used to buy supplies and books. You may even have more adventurous plans like opening a savings account and each member putting in $50 a month to go toward a shared trip away to a sacred site at the end of the year. There are often local retreats and festivals happening that you may also wish to attend as a group. Check out the websites at the end of this book to find out information on various festivals and gatherings.

For bigger trips you may want to venture to the South— New Orleans is fabulous, with its Voodoo museums and mysterious swamplands, and in the Northeast, Salem, the site of the infamous Salem Witch Trials, is an obvious choice! Here you can visit the Craft store of famous Witch Laurie Cabot (read her book *The Power of the Witch*—I highly recommend it), and maybe she will cook up a personal spell for you. Taos in New Mexico and the Joshua Tree in the Californian desert are other amazing spiritual hotspots. Closer to my home, magickal Topanga Canyon in the hills above Malibu Beach is like stepping back in time to the halcyon days of the hippy!

There are plenty of ways of getting money together for coven magickal excursions and bigger expenses (like perhaps hiring a space to have a permanently set-up altar and circle). Garage sales, selling items you have made (like magickal soaps and incense blends) at Pagan festivals and gatherings, or even putting a band together and doing shows and putting all the proceeds into the coven petty cash fund are some ideas.

It's as simple as that. However, you may like to examine why you feel uncomfortable, and if it is something to do with not being proud of your body or being uncomfortable in your skin, then you may like to do some self-love rituals to affirm and appreciate your unique physical beauty.

I never charge money to teach the Craft or magickally help people, but occasionally, if I am conducting a public workshop and it has cost me money to travel and obtain accommodation, I will charge a fee to cover those expenses. When I do a spell or ritual for someone and they are happy with the results, I suggest they make a donation to a charity of their choice or donate some of their time to a worthy cause.

I get comments from people like, "You must be so rich with all your books and doing spells for people." Practicing the Craft and helping and teaching people actually end up costing me more than I make personally. But that's cool; my point is that money should never come between you and your Craft. If chipping in a few dollars and appointing someone to keep track of the expenses suits everyone, then do it. If not, keep it fairly relaxed like I do in my coven. Some will say that money is energy and Witches work with energy, and as such they have no qualms charging for their witchy services. Certainly in my case, when I spend hours on the Internet answering questions and holding workshops teaching the Craft I am using up the time I would normally spend earning money. But I find that spiritual energy runs purer without money involved.

Incorporating As a Church

If you are interested in incorporating your coven as a business and benefiting from the various tax exemptions that being a church provides, I suggest you contact a good accountant and get expert advice.

Rite Now!

Your first coven meeting doesn't need to be a nerve-racking nightmare! With planning and a sense of adventure (and humor!), you can have a marvelous, intense experience that gets your coven off to a great start. In this chapter I will outline the basic skills of casting a circle, summoning the elements, invoking the Goddess and God, raising power, closing the circle, and then the feasting and grounding of excess energies that occur afterwards. I have written how to do this in my other books, but honestly, after years of practice, I find there is no one "correct" technique for casting a circle and doing all of the above. Different techniques suit different purposes, different times, and different people. Of course, if you are working within a tradition, like Gardnerian or Dianic, you would always use the methods required by their teachings. When you are working in an eclectic coven, however, the one thing that is "correct" and indeed imperative is that every covener has the same comprehension of what is being done. The greatest strength of a coven (and one of the main reasons for forming one) is the group mind that can be created and its strength. So when you choose your coven's circlecasting ritual, make sure everyone understands what the symbols mean, and make sure that they emotionally connect with the words used to invoke the God/dess and that you are all fused in intent and desire.

First, though, I'm going to talk about what comes before the spiritual ceremony. Important stuff like . . .

Making It Real

One way to ensure a really powerful and transformational gathering is to write your circlecasting ritual, elemental and God/dess invocations, and power-raising chants yourself. I did this for my coven. Now you might say, "But Fiona! You've been a Witch for ages—it's easy for you to think up stuff!" But really it's not hard and the buzz you get from writing your own words helps you to really connect with what you are trying to do.

Focusing on the Task at Hand

As I have pointed out, my coven has an agreement that we don't talk about personal stuff before we start the ritual. We leave all that for later, during the grounding and feasting. When we enter the space selected for our ritual we leave the everyday world behind. We keep talking to a minimum and get straight into being magickal.

Help! What If I Get Nervous?

I still get a bit nervous at times; if it's been a while since my coven has gathered, my mouth gets a bit dry. This is because I want it to be good for everyone! But if nerves strike, or if you're starting out and you feel a little bit silly or not connected, say that you need a moment. Take a deep breath and close your eyes, go inward, and connect with that deep sense of perfect self. Be in the moment, at one with your intent. Know that you are everything you desire to be. Your time is now. Take another breath, open your eyes, and . . .

Cast the Circle

When you cast a circle, you are creating a sacred space that can contain energies you want and keep out energies you don't want. You shape it like a sphere, around you, above you, and below you. The "realness" of it will depend on how strongly you can all imagine it into being. When I conduct spell-casting parties and open coven meetings, I cast the circle and explain to everyone what we are doing. Even though most of the people are not experienced Witches, there is still a very tangible circle being cast because everyone is focused on the same thing. Being focused is the key to success: that and taking it seriously and believing in what you are doing. Then the magickal things you create can take on a life of their own.

An example of this is when I did a spellcasting party for a news anchor in Los Angeles. We cast the circle in her living room: there was a mixed group of men and women (about thirteen of us total), and I was the only Witch. We did various spells together within the circle and then we walked around the house as a group, blessing it. We stepped outside to bless the garden, and on re-entering the house, my eyes immediately went out of focus. I was looking at the area where we had all sat and cast the circle together. It was blurry. I looked through the archway into another room and my vision was clear. I looked back to the living room area and it was blurry again. The cast circle was so tangible that the skeptic that still occasionally lurks within me was shocked. Interestingly, I had cast the circle to encompass the whole house, but I expect that all the "Witchlings" had created it to exist exactly where we had all sat together. And when we walked away from it in the physical world, it stayed happily glued together, fused with our desire and intent.

The point of telling you all this is to get you excited about creating a sacred space. It's real, it's special, and it's one of the most wonderful witchy things you can learn to do, because it means you can build your church anywhere, anytime.

The basic action of casting the circle is pretty similar, no matter what book you read. You stand and point either your athame, wand, index finger, feather, or whatever you are using, and see light streaming out from the point. You then trace this light in a circle around you, moving in a sunwise direction, which is clockwise in the Northern Hemisphere and counterclockwise in the Southern

Enchanting Numbers

0: Perfect love and
perfect trust

1: The empowered self

2: The perfect couple

3: Positive and
personal power

4: Balance and harmony

5: Physical and
mental strength

6: Love and passion

7: Spiritual enlightenment

8: Infinite potential

9: Wisdom and
power

Hemisphere. I'll explain: in the Southern Hemisphere, the sun rises in the east and sets in the west, but it veers north as it does this, thus tracing a counterclockwise arc across the sky. In the Northern Hemisphere it veers south, describing a clockwise arc.

You may find that many books (especially older ones) state that circles have to be marked in white paint, chalk, or rope and must be exactly nine feet in circumference and aligned with the four points of the compass. In my early days I put off casting a circle for ages because I was so worried about getting all the measurements right. There is indeed a numerological significance in having a circle of nine feet. It's the number nine that is important: so it could be nine feet, nine inches, or even nine nautical miles! Nine is the number of power and wisdom. You can utilize the power of numbers in your circle-casting if you want—or not.

In our coven gatherings I usually put out a circle of tealight candles in glass jars so that they don't get knocked over and splash wax or blow out if we're outside. To harness the power of numbers, I may place nine candles for wisdom, eight for potential, seven for enlightenment, and so on. But I'm not too concerned about having a physical form of our circle, as we create it between the worlds anyway. But hey, it looks good and it adds to the atmosphere, which can certainly increase our powers of imagination and visualization. As an added bonus, the element of fire is a powerful catalyst for change and empowerment.

In my coven's Book of Shadows we have written:

> *The perimeter of the circle is created by the energy channeled by the athame, which shall be visualized by the coveners as blue/white light. It can also be physically marked out by salt, a tracing in the earth, or a ring of candles.*

Invocation of the Circle

The wording for this is always pretty simple but potent. The person casting the circle stands with their athame, wand, or finger raised and all the coveners focus hard on "seeing" the blue/white light pour from the tip of the blade to trace a circle around them. This then splits into bands of light above and below their feet, forming the sphere. When the tracing is complete, the circlecaster then traces a large pentagram over the circle and seals the process. As the circle is being cast and the pentagram is traced, the following kind of invocation should be used:

Tracing the Circle

I conjure our circle so that it may exist between the worlds,

a potent place of magick and infinite potential.

Tracing the Pentagram

The circle is bound and blessed.

So mote it be.

One person usually does the action, but everyone can say the words together if you like. I generally lead our coven though the process with actions and spoken words as Tri and Zorrita concentrate on visualizing the circle form. One of the reasons why I most often lead is because I am more experienced, but I think it's important to share leadership roles within the coven as the member's individual wisdom and experience evolves. Doing this encourages everyone to be proactive and involved and thus keeps the workings more potent.

Witch Tip

The world manifests according to the way you see it. Understanding this is your greatest magickal tool. Your imagination can really become reality—tangible, physical reality. There are many levels of manifestation. Some younger folk may get scared by this and think, "Well, if I imagine a monster, then it will exist!" However, know this: the things you imagine only have as much power over you as you give them. You imagined them, so in a sense you created them;

A Note on Writing Your Own Stuff

Here's an example of where you could get creative. Why not start your circle invocation as "I conjure thee, circle, so that you may exist between the worlds," and then add your own description, perhaps something like "vibrant and potent, ripe with our dreams and desires."

Remember that the words need to inspire and excite you so that you and your coveners feel ready for anything—anything magickal, that is!

Okay, the Circle Is Cast— What's Next?

Next you need to introduce the physical elements of magickal manifestation into the circle. By this I mean air, earth, fire, and water.

A lot of books (including my earlier ones) will talk about summoning the Guardians of the Watchtowers and seeing metaphysical beings like sylphs (for air), undines (for water), salamanders (for fire), and gnomes (for earth) dwelling in the corresponding quarters of your circle. This is all perfectly fine and valid, and when you really connect with these entities you are tapping into a collective, unconscious projection. In a sense they do exist, as thousands of others have imagined them into existence before you. These methods and descriptions are derivative of Gardnerian magickal practices, which in themselves are derivative of Masonic rituals. Now, personally

I don't put a human (or human-like) form to the elements. In my coven we reinforce the qualities that the elements represent to us, and we visualize them in their natural state.

You may also read in other books that different colored candles are required to be placed in each quarter relating to the qualities of the elements being invoked. This is working with color magick and is certainly a valid and enforced practice in certain traditions. However, in an eclectic coven, we place objects that relate to the natural state of the element in the corresponding quarters of the altar.

From our Book of Shadows:

The following are placed on the altar:
East/air: incense (or a feather if we can't have smoke)
South/fire: a lit candle (or unlit if we can't have a flame)
West/water: a bowl of water with a pinch of salt and
a seashell
North/earth: a crystal

Please note that these are Northern Hemisphere correspondences. In the Southern Hemisphere, place the fire in the north and the earth in the south.

There are various reasons for aligning the four elements with the four points of the compass. One of those reasons is certainly that if you align yourself with the earth's electromagnetic poles, you will harness more power for your magickal use. Another reason, for example, is if you are on the west coast of a landmass and there is a large body of water to the

their presence is only fueled by your continual acknowledgement of their existence. This idea is aligned with what I have said in this book about creating a covenworld that exists whether your coven members are physically in the same space or not. If you all get slack and don't reinforce its existence, its energy will dissipate. In the same way, if you create a thoughtform that spooks you, stop thinking about it and it will cease to have any effect on you and go away.

west, then it makes sense to have water in the west quarter. But, to be honest, after years of casting a circle (and this differs from what I wrote in my first book), I have really connected with the concept that you are casting a circle "between the worlds" and the physical laws of this earthly realm should not bind you. Following are the ways I relate to the directions of the compass and the elements that "reside" in those quarters.

Air in the East

The sun rises in the east, and just as it rises there is usually a breeze that eases across the land like the waking breath of the world. Night has ended and a brand-new day means a brand-new beginning. Air is the element we relate to change (the winds of change) and refreshing, renewing energies. So it connects with me to use air for the east. And connection is what it's all about—your connection and comprehension of what you're doing is what makes real magick.

Fire in the South

I spend most of my time in the Northern Hemisphere now, and I have become very connected with experiencing fire in the south. There is a physical reason for this: the heat of the equator, the hottest part of the planet that revolves closest to the sun, is to the south. When I was living in Australia, the equator was to the north. Now this begs the question, of course: what if you live in Fiji, which is virtually on top of the equator? Perhaps you'd invoke fire in the center of the circle. This illustrates my point that getting too pedantic about which quarter should have which element is a waste of magickal energy. Just get the elemental energies in there in a way that is meaningful and moving for you and your coveners.

Water in the West

The sun sets in the west and so signifies an ending, but also a beginning: day and night transform from one to the other again. To me, the element of water brings to mind the tides of the oceans—as everything flows in, so it must flow out, like cycles of emotions, like cycles of life, like the cycles of the rising and setting sun. As much as 70 percent of our physical makeup is water, and water magickally represents emotions, whether in ritual or in dreams. The end of the day is an emotional time, so having water in the west, the quarter of the setting sun, is meaningful to me.

Earth in the North

Again, like fire, earth in the north is an obvious physical reference. In the Northern Hemisphere, we look away from the equator to the contemplative coolness of the North Pole, and this reflects earth. I relate to the poles, being magnetic, as having an anchoring effect. And that is effectively the role that the element of earth plays in a magickal circle; it anchors our efforts in the physical realm. So the poles of north (if you're in the Northern Hemisphere) and south (if you're in the Southern Hemisphere) perfectly represent earth.

Invocation of the Elements

As each element is called, the coveners turn to face the corresponding direction and the object is held up and interacted with to empower the ritual. Incense is fanned with a hand or feather for air; the candle is raised to cast its light over the proceedings for fire; water is sprinkled from fingertips; and crystal is touched to the ground for earth.

I open the quarter of air to inspire our dreams and lift our spirits.

I open the quarter of fire to fuel our goals and empower our workings.

I open the quarter of water to fill our hearts and nourish our potential.

I open the quarter of earth to anchor our efforts in the physical realm.

Again, like in casting a circle, everyone can say the words together. In my coven I say the words and do the actions, and the coveners chime little Tibetan bells as each element is invoked.

A Note on Writing Your Own Elemental Invocations

Based on what I have explained about the qualities of the elements, you might like to write your own descriptions of what they represent to you and the imagery that will best inspire you, and so create a more effective portal for them to manifest in the circle. One of the things I enjoy most about doing witchy workshops and open gatherings is inviting everyone to create their own invocations. We have a chat about what the elements represent, and then I invite people to write their own interpretations. Often they are really beautiful and moving, and when we use them to call the elements everyone is elevated and at one with the element as it manifests. So you can use my coven's invocations if you like, or let your imagination run wild and write something special!

Honoring the Goddess and the God

In certain traditions, the Goddess and God are acknowledged and asked to enter into the circle by the circlecaster calling on "the Lord and Lady" or sometimes specific names like "Isis and Osiris." In some traditions, only the Goddess is called: "Triple Goddess—Maiden, Mother, Crone—avail us of your presence and bless us with your assistance."

Being an unconventional Witch, I don't believe that the Goddess and God exist in a human-like form independent of our acknowledgement and recognition. However, I do relate to the concept of the collective unconscious and feel I can access archetypes and projected thoughtforms of divinity that have evolved along with the development of culture and society in human life. Relating to goddesses and gods in this way by no means diminishes their spiritual relevance to me. If anything, it makes them more relevant, accessible, and real, because what we create our goddesses and gods to be are expressions of interaction with the divine concept that I do believe in: life itself. By shaping the amorphous and enormous energy of the life force into gods and goddesses, we can experience our innate universal magnificence.

Witches honor that the feminine and masculine principles of divinity are capable of being expressed in either gender. To reflect this, when my coven invokes the Goddess and God, we acknowledge that they are present within us at all times, and we honor them by honoring ourselves within the circle.

To invoke the Goddess and God, each covener touches their heart (body) and forehead (mind), and circles their arms outward (spirit) as they intone:

I declare the Goddess and God manifest in circle

Present in my body, mind, and spirit.

At this point, if the coven is dedicated to a particular goddess and/or god, they can be invoked independently using an agreed-upon invocation and ritual. My coven is dedicated to Lilith, who originated in approximately 2300 BCE as an all-powerful, feminist, Sumerian goddess and was later absorbed into the Hebrew and Muslim religions. Upon this, sadly, she went from being a holy and remarkable expression of feminine power to being debased as the evil first wife of Adam who was cast out of Eden, and then being further demoted to demon by the Levite priests who wrote the Bible. Certainly she's one hell of a woman! Together we invoke her in her original exalted form by passionately saying the following passage that I wrote:

Winged goddess of the dawn and night,

Bathe us in your dark light.

We Witches gather in your sight

Sharing your eternal flight.

You can write the invocation of your god/dess to best describe what they represent to you and thus have a more potent form of them manifest in your circle. To us, Lilith is omnipresent, day and night, light and dark. She waxes and wanes in presence, reflecting the coming and going of all things, the expanding and contracting of our lungs, the ebb and flow of the ocean, the heave and sway of universal energies, the beginning and ending of our lives. Her dark spirit of enlightenment is expressed in the heavens: it has to be dark to see the stars. Her sight is upon all things and within all things. Her eternal flight from the repressive and elitist Garden of Eden and the rigid demands of the patriarchal system is representative of the pure freedom of spirit that all women and men deserve, and her wings beat the breath of beauty and sensual love into all things.

Spend some time getting to know your chosen god/dess and fall in love with them so that they explode into your circle when you call, their manifestation fueled by your love and appreciation of them (and yourselves)!

The Circle Is Cast and Plump with Potent Energies . . . Now What?

Now you can get down to performing the specific tasks, rituals, or spells that you want to cast in the sacred space. Ritual work and spellcasting is not about putting on Academy Award-winning performances—it's about being magickal. Of course there is always an element of theater in ritual, with the words and gestures and the way they are experienced by others in circle, but don't get so caught up in the role-playing that you are numb to the feeling. Conversely, though, if the words and actions are what get you excited, go for broke! I guess I'm just encouraging you not to get put off when you read in some books really elaborate "acts" with "scripts" prescribing what you have to do to celebrate a sabbat or perform a healing ritual. It's important that you read and understand the lesson in what these wordy and complicated rituals are imparting, but once you have extracted the essence and fully comprehended it, then you can set out expressing its magick in your and your coven's own unique way.

Here's a really good tip for successful spellcasting and ritual work at any time, and especially when you're working in a group: it's the KISS theory (and it's got nothing to do with Paul Stanley and Gene Simmons, though they are friends of mine!). It simply means Keep It Simple, Sorceress/er!

A simple ritual performed with confidence and passion will pack a far greater magickal punch than a complicated performance that is convoluted, disjointed, and ebbs and flows in intensity as people scramble to remember their lines and moves. Of course, as you become more experienced, it will be a challenge and indeed fun to create more evolved and complicated rituals. But in the early stages, think KISS!

Raising Power

Generally any spellcasting or ritual work taking place in the circle will involve raising power to add fuel to the vehicle of the magickal transformation taking place. It certainly is one of the reasons you have a circle—to contain the energies you raise so that they are like arrows, pulled right back in a well-strung bow, before you release them, *pow!*, to do their work.

Cone of Power

A cone of power is a spinning mass of energy built by the coveners to fuel spells along their way. Music, chanting, drumming, physically running around, breathing—anything really, as long as it's done passionately, rhythmically, and with unified intent, will raise the cone of power within the circle until it is released.

In my coven we raise power by chanting our goddess chant: "Lilith, Lilith, Lilith!" We will chant this over and over again, starting softly and then getting louder and louder until our hair is standing up on the back of our necks and our bodies are tingling all over. Until you have experienced raising a cone of power, you can't really imagine how intense and tangible it feels—nor how intense and tangible it feels when you release it to fuel the spell you have just cast. It really does feel like an enormous *whoosh* of energy!

You can release the power a number of ways. Often we will hold our joined hands slightly aloft and then, as the cone peaks, throw them to the sky. Then together we call:

By one, this spell is done

By two, it shall come true

By three, so must it be

By four, for the good of all

By five, our dreams come alive!

As we call "alive!" we each visualize the circle parting over our heads, creating a vortex. In my mind's eye, I see the energy speeding away through layers of reality to do its work.

Sometimes we don't say anything to "cap it off." If we are not holding hands, we just stop in unison and I use my athame to cut a large pentagram into the top of the circle. We visualize the power spiraling out like rapidly swirling smoke, taking our magickal intentions with it to manifest in the physical world at the appropriate time.

Looking up and cutting a pentagram vortex into the top of the circle sometimes strikes me as a bit predictable, because we are so conditioned to look toward the heavens when doing anything exalted or involving power. If we honor the earth, why do we not look down to the ground under our feet? It's just as holy, sacred, and divine as the sky above our heads. Looking up when we chant or pray implies that divinity is separate from us—above our heads and out of our reach—and that we have to appeal to its good favor (you can tell I was brought up as a Catholic). You and your coven might like to experiment with looking *down* to focus power and cutting a hole in the bottom of the circle so that the magick rushes out that way. (This is especially a good idea if you are doing healing spells and rituals for the environment.)

Generally, though, I find looking up to be appropriate, but it's important to think about *why* you are looking up. Not because the God/dess is in the sky out of our reach, lording over us and looking down on us, but because a celestial view and vision is refreshing, awe-inspiring, and connected to our crown chakras, the uppermost energy center of our body that more often than not faces the sky.

Totally Charged: Potent Power-Raising Techniques

Music

Music is the voice of the soul, and music that is powerful, evocative, and has intense rhythms and lots of emotion is a perfect way to raise power in a circle. Believe it or not, for a long time I would put on tracks by bands like Metallica, Slayer, and Godsmack to raise power during my solitary rituals.

Witch Tip

Think about what you're doing and why. If you have a direct, personal relationship with every magickal action you take, then it will be powerful magick that you can trust will work.

Always choose a track that excites your coveners. Close your eyes, hold hands, and together "feelualize" (different from *visualize*—i.e., feel the music course through you all), churning up your chakras as you generate a throbbing cone of power. This is a really cool way to raise power!

Another way to raise power is by actually performing the music together. Now generally this only works if you are already reasonably accomplished musicians, with enough musical chemistry that will create the shift and push of energy required to create a cone of power. But you can chant, sing, and/or drum together to raise power even if you are not the next Wolfmother!

Chanting

As I have mentioned already, you can chant your unique god/dess chant that you have created for your coven or perhaps just the name of your patron god/dess. Familiarity with it is important, but to be honest, you get very used to it after you've chanted it over thirty times to raise power! The Wiccan Goddess Chant is a classic that I first read in Starhawk's brilliant work *The Spiral Dance*. It is the names of some of the most loved goddesses from different cultures looped together poetically:

Isis, Astarte, Diana, Hecate, Demeter, Kali, Inanna

Note: Diana is pronounced "Dee–anna" and Hecate is pronounced "Hek–atte" (as in "latte") so that it all rolls off the tongue smoothly.

You can also chant the names of your coveners over and over again, or a word or short sentence that relates to the purpose and goal of your ritual or spell. Anything really, as long as it can be said faster and faster without tongue-tying everyone!

Singing

A capella singing of inspirational words is another wonderful way to raise power. Choosing a chorus from a favorite song and singing it over and over again with more and more feeling will raise power. However, you need to be aware that for really effective cones of power, there is a hypnotic, rhythmic effect necessary, shifting the spellcasters from a beta mind state to an alpha one or, if they are well-practiced, a theta mind state.

Meditative Mind States

Alpha, beta, theta. . .?
These are names for
different types of brain
waves that represent
different states of
consciousness.

Beta is the fastest frequency. This is the brain wave we
use when we're operating
in the everyday, regular
world: running to the bus
stop, speaking to friends,
and working.

Alpha is the next brain
wave that is slower and is
what we project when we
are relaxing, whether we
are looking at a beautiful
sunset or consciously
meditating. Our bodies
respond to this state by our
heart rate slowing and our
general sense of well-being
improving. We feel content.

Drumming

This is a favorite for many Witches. Small drums, struck with
sticks or hands, are wonderfully hypnotic and raise excellent
cones of power. It's not even necessary for it to sound good.
As long as it captures an intensity of passion of spirit, then it
will do the job and raise the cone of power.

Breath Toning

Breathing in and then breathing out audibly with a big "oooh"
sound can work well as long as you don't hyperventilate and
pass out! I have used this method as a solitary Witch but not
in a group yet, though I often draw attention to the fact that
when we are gathering as a coven, we are breathing in the
breath that has been in each other's lungs. In a way it's like
making love—the intimacy of sharing breath, when acknowledged and focused upon, is a beautiful and powerful expression of unity.

Physical Movement

If you have a lot of room, physically running around in a circle
is a good way to raise power and brings to mind a fun vision
of wild Witches in long black robes holding hands and running around a large bubbling cauldron! Of course the athletic nature of this will depend on an individual's comfort and
fitness. Often, though, coven meetings are held in enclosed
spaces like people's living rooms, which rules out lots of physical movement.

Earthing the Power

After you have raised a cone of power and released it to do its work, it's usual to feel a residue still in the circle. You may feel light-headed or tingly or even slightly unsettled, so you need to earth the power. A good way to do this is simply for all the co-veners to place their hands on the ground together and visual-ize the residue draining out of them into the welcoming earth, or you can stand and consciously channel it through your feet.

Closing the Circle

Once you have completed your ritual and/or spellcasting ac-tivities, you can wind up the proceedings by closing the circle. In some books you will read that at this point you must have a "cakes and ale" (food and drink) ceremony. There is a twofold purpose for this: one, to honor the Goddess and God, and two, to help ground any excess energies in the coveners from the magickal work just undertaken.

In my coven we usually leave the cakes and ale ceremony until after we have closed the circle. If we have invoked a par-ticular goddess or god for ritual work or have invoked our patron god/dess, it is now that we "thank and farewell" them. For example:

> Thank you, Hecate, queen of the crossroads,
>
> Greek goddess of the night,
>
> For witnessing, blessing, and assisting our rite.
>
> We bid you hail and farewell until next in circle we dwell.

Theta is the brain wave we use when we are working in the magickal realm. It is slower again and means that our subconscious is accessed and we are in a visionary and often profoundly spiritual state of awareness. This is the state that magickal work most often evokes.

There is one more really slow brain wave and that is **delta**. Delta usually means you're deeply asleep or even unconscious. This state can be brought on consciously by those very practiced at deep meditation like some yogis, healers, and Witches!

Then we again honor the God/dess made manifest within us personally by each stating:

I am Goddess and God,

I honor my divinity.

I thank the powers within and without

For assisting and blessing me.

Releasing the Elements

The elemental energies that you welcomed into your circle (air, fire, water, and earth) need to now be formally released. You will read in some books that they have to be "farewelled" individually with elaborate pentagrams cut into the circle so that they can be dispersed. In our coven we release them in one motion by tracing a pentagram into either the top or bottom of the circle sphere with an athame and intoning:

We honor the elements and their assistance.

Hail and farewell until next in circle we dwell.

As the pentagram is traced, we all visualize the energies dispersing. I always feel a shift in the energy of the circle when we do this—like it's been given a jiggle and everything is starting to loosen up.

Next, the circle should be opened. Using the athame, trace an energy line at the edge of the sphere in an "against the sun" movement (which is counterclockwise in the Northern Hemisphere and clockwise in the Southern Hemisphere) so that it disperses, and say the following words:

The circle is open but unbroken.

The circle is open but unbroken.

The circle is open but unbroken,

Carried within our hearts.

Always merry meet and always merry part.

Feasting

As noted in our Book of Shadows: "Food and drink must always be consumed after circle to ground energies and enhance coveners' bonding in the physical realm."

In eating and drinking, we "earth" ourselves. Sometimes, depending on how intense the magickal work was, you can feel quite lightheaded and like you have butterflies in your stomach. If you try to go to bed and sleep like that, you will lie awake all night or have strange, unsettling dreams. We usually have a good chat after everything and discuss our impressions of the ritual. If we have cast a specific spell, however, we don't chat about it. To repeat an analogy I often use: when you cast a spell it's like planting a seed—you don't keep digging it up to see how it's going. So we will discuss our overall impressions but not analyze any of the specific proceedings.

If it's a sabbat, we usually spend quite a bit of time eating and drinking together and talking. After a full moon gathering or specific ritual, it's usually just a cup of tea and a cookie. We always crumble a little of the food on the earth and pour a little of our drink also on the earth as an offering and libation to the Goddess (within and without us). Sometimes if we're indoors, gathering at one of our apartments, the person whose place it is will collect some crumbs and drink after everyone has left and perform the libations then.

Checklist for Coven Meeting Structure

After all that information, I thought I should break it down into a relatively simple checklist for you:

Planning the Coven Meeting

1. Decide to hold a gathering.

2. Email/phone the coveners to ensure everyone's attendance.

3. Decide on a location or venue that is accessible, private, safe, and secure.

4. Write/copy the purpose and outline of the ritual, the suggested magickal tools for the co-veners to bring, and the appropriate magickal attire to wear. Either email or fax this to each covener so that everyone is familiar with the intent and any necessary invocations or chants for the ritual.

5. Buy or gather any specific ingredients for spells or the ritual.

6. On the day, prepare the space and set up the altar. If you like, create a physical demarcation of the circle.

Performing the Coven Meeting

1. Cast the circle.

2. Call on the four elements.

3. Honor the Goddess and God as they exist within the coveners, and call on a specific goddess or god if your ritual requires it.

4. Perform your ritual and/or spellcasting.

5. Raise a cone of power to fuel the ritual/spell.

6. Ground any residue of the cone of power by placing your hands on the ground or channeling it out through the soles of your feet.

7. Thank and farewell any specific god/dess you invoked, and again honor the Goddess and God as manifest within the hearts, minds, and spirits of the coveners.

8. Release the four elements.

9. Open the circle.

10. Eat, drink, and be merry!

Keep a Record

It's important that you keep dated records of all your covenwork in your Book of Shadows. Generally I write up the rituals before the gathering, and sometimes I ask my coveners to research a certain topic or to write a contribution to the ritual—usually a poem or ode to the Goddess. This is where we Witches practicing the ancient craft of magick embrace modern technology with enthusiasm! I can email the girls updates and outlines of gatherings so they are prepped beforehand, and then I print out the outline of the ritual and simply paste it in our Book of Shadows.

Once I used to be very pedantic and felt that everything had to be copied out by hand. And indeed in some traditions it is common to have each coven initiate copy the coven's Book of Shadows by hand in order to process and assimilate the knowledge. However, I think making this a prerequisite could lead to shoddy Book of Shadows-keeping. Our lives are far more complicated and busy than they would have been fifty years ago, when this idea started with some of the early traditional groups. I don't think there's anything wrong with printing out information and emailing web links amongst coven members when an interesting article on Goddess worship or magick is discovered on the Internet. It's all just a sign of the times. However, as I mention in the chapter "Let's Get Going," it's important to personalize your Book of Shadows. My coven marked it with our blood and hand-wrote odes to our goddess, Lilith. As well, I paste in the pages of our ritual work, photos and cool images that we find of Lilith, and anything else that is appropriate.

As I said at the start of this chapter, your first coven gathering doesn't have to be a nightmare. Likewise, ensuing coven gatherings don't have to become perfunctory or repetitive. Always think about what you are all doing, be creative, and trust in your coven's magickal potential—this will ensure that your covenworld evolves to be always lush, challenging, and exciting.

Dedicate Your Coven

Your first coven gathering is likely to be the dedication of your coven. I say "likely" because it's not essential; in fact, you might like to have a couple of "practice sessions" before you have the very important dedication ceremony. In my coven, the first gathering happened to be in front of television cameras! This may sound like we are exhibitionists, but there was actually a fair reason for our overt behavior. At the time, I was pitching a television show to the networks about real-life Witchcraft (as opposed to what you see on *Charmed* and *Sabrina*). I wanted to film an example of a real gathering of Witches performing a ritual, and my new coven members were kind enough to say that we could do a trial run in front of the cameras.

I kept a diary of this whole experience—I'll share it with you!

10 September 2002

Showtime! It's kind of bizarre having your first coven meeting in front of television cameras. Well, it wasn't really an official meeting, more like a practice run that we agreed to film at my house for a segment on my new TV show. It was very rewarding because there is an element of performance in every ritual, and we three girls really got a sense of how meaningful theatrics can enhance a magickal experience. We made sure we memorized our lines and knew our invocation gestures—which is exactly what you should do for a real coven meeting. It was particularly good for Tri and Zorrita (as they are less experienced than I am) to dress rehearse for the real event in a couple of weeks: Mabon, the Autumn Equinox, is when we will be dedicating our coven for real. For the ritual part of the meeting, we did a banishing spell for Tri on someone who seems not to have understood her need for privacy. She is absolutely fed up, and we agreed that it would be appropriate to banish the person "for the good of all, with harm to none." In doing this, we would not be interfering with their free will (a no-no in Witchcraft) but helping them to move on, which is surely doing them a service!

You should have seen the look on the director's and cameraman's faces when we pulled out the red candle, cast in the shape of a naked man, and proceeded to light it, proclaiming loudly, "We banish you from bothering Tri, for the good of all, this is our decree!" The energy that Tri, Zorrita, and I raised felt really potent, and when Zorrita started playing her accordion—long, slow, sensual notes that Tri and I swayed to in unison as we chanted—the guys' eyes were popping out of their heads!

At the end of the ritual the director said, "God, I better do a good job of editing this—I don't want to upset you girls and be on the receiving end of a spell like that!" I reminded him that it was "for the good of all, with harm to none," and we were much more likely to do a nice spell for him than a nasty one! I have to say I was impressed with the overall comments I later got from the TV crew, particularly from one guy who said that he didn't really know what to expect when he accepted the job to film a group of Witches. He suspected it was all going to be gimmicky, Elvira-style special effects, but he told me that he found everything that we said really thought-provoking. He said it made a lot of sense, especially when we spoke about respecting the earth and working with its ener-gies, and acknowledged that men and women embody divine consciousness. He said he had goose bumps when we did the spell, which was surprising because he thought it would all be rubbish. But he went on to say that he realized it's easy to be cynical when you haven't actually experienced some-thing magickal and now that he had, it had opened his eyes in a way that almost freaked him out, the whole experience was so powerful.

When all the television people had left, Tri, Zorrita, and I had a group hug and agreed that we were onto something really exciting. We have come such a long way in the short month since our initial meeting at the coffee shop in Venice, but there is still lots more to do before Mabon. We agreed to meet on Friday to flesh out the final plans for our formal coven dedication ceremony.

I must add that a few weeks later I asked Tri about the banishing spell and how it had worked for her, and she said she had burnt the candle and buried the remains and hadn't been bothered since. Nothing negative seemed to have come of the spell, so it's safe to assume that, as we hoped, the spell helped the other person too, in that they moved on with their own life.

Here is an email I sent to the girls after our TV ritual. I am including it to illustrate the steps you can take in planning your coven dedication. Again, good planning and preparation is essential for the event to be significantly powerful and magickal.

From: Fiona Horne
Sent: Thursday, 12 September, 2002 8:37 pm
To: Tri, Zorrita
Subject: Lilith Coven Dedication Timeline

Task List for Coven Dedication
Date for Dedication: Mabon—Autumn Equinox
8:55 pm, Sunday, 22 September 2002

Tuesday 17 through to Thursday 19 September
Please have a good read of the notes on circlecasting I gave you yesterday. Also, please review the notes on Lilith I gave you last week to familiarize yourself with who she is and what she represents.

Friday, 20 September
We will need to have coffee together to run through the ritual and work out what each of us needs to bring. I will give you our special Lilith Coven chant that we will need to have memorized for the dedication. Also we have to write a personal declaration of commitment and intent to the coven; it only needs to be a paragraph or two.

Sunday, 22 September
7 pm: Tri and Zorrita to get ready at Zorrita's after work. Fiona to meet them there at 7:30. Dress should be black and of opulent appearance; makeup and hair should be elaborate, i.e., dress up! But also be comfortable, as we will be on a beach or in another natural place.
7:30–8: Drive to location for coven dedication.
8–8:55: Preparation of location, tracing circle, setting up altar, brief rehearsal of ritual.
8:55: Dedication of Lilith Coven.
10: Late dinner together on the beach or at a restaurant (if we go to Malibu, there are restaurants across the road).
11:30: Home in bed!

Tri, Zorrita, and I met on Friday evening to discuss the ritual and exchange information. Here is my diary entry from this night (for a little meeting at a coffee shop, it was quite an interesting night)!

20 September 2002

Met Tri and Zorrita at the Coffee Bean and Tea Leaf in Beverly Hills. Tri was a bit late, but it was good because it gave Zorrita and me the chance to go over her coven goals—basically what she wanted to achieve by being in the coven. She is particularly interested in shamanic work: embodying the spirit of various animals to experience their unique talents and wisdom. She is drawn to the wolf, which is great synchronicity since I had recently ordered a real wolf's heart to be the coven's power talisman and totem. (Freeze-dried and harvested from a wolf who died of natural causes on a reservation. I got it from Panpipes Magickal Marketplace on Cahuenga and Hollywood. I love going into this store—they have the most unique items!) The wolf is such an amazing animal, so tenacious and strong, and these are the qualities that a new coven really needs to stay together for the long haul.

Tri arrived (she'd been held up at work), and we started fine-tuning the dedication ritual. I had been up until two in the morning the night before, typing up my suggestions, and the girls were really happy with my notes. Because I am the most experienced it's appropriate that I lead at this stage, but as far as I'm concerned, leadership is established so it can be shared. I reminded the girls to memorize the circlecasting ritual because I would do it the first few times but then it would be their turn! As we drank our coffees and ate our muffins, our conversation spanned such topics as animal parts, goddess names, and the best and most hygienic ways to stamp our blood thumbprint in our coven Book of Shadows on the night of the dedication. We agreed that, as much as we loved each other, when being magickal you also have to be practical, so we decided the best way to prick our thumbs would be with safe individual thumb prickers bought from the drug store, the kind that diabetics use to test their insulin levels. It's important that we make a blood offering on that night, to really seal our intent and commitment to the coven. It occurred to me as we were chatting that I wondered what the other people in the coffee shop would think if they knew there were a bunch of Witches sitting in the corner talking about animal parts and blood offerings! Especially the group to our left, who were Christian and holding a Bible meeting! They were loudly praying and discussing fundamentalist aspects of the Bible. It was quite a surreal moment—in all the hundreds of times I've been into a coffee shop, I've never seen a Bible meeting. How bizarre that it happened to be the night we were having a coven meeting!

When I got home, I looked at the new, long list of things I needed to do as coven leader and wondered how I would fit all these tasks into my busy work schedule. I realize that it's quite a massive job to establish a coven, much like running your own church, but I know it's really going to be worth it. Already I feel an enormous amount of love for my beautiful witchy sisters, and every day I get more and more excited about the adventure we are embarking upon together.

I didn't keep any more diary entries after this because I got really busy staying on top of everything that needed to be done before our coven dedication, as well as working to promote a new book I had out at the time. The dedication was an amazing event and I want to share it with you, as I hope it will inspire you as you go about creating your own. I did not get the following proceedings out of a book—I followed my heart, trusted my intuition, and created an event that was unique and meaningful and therefore more powerful. It will give you an idea of what can go on at your dedication, but what ultimately does is up to you . . .

Finding an appropriate place for the coven dedication was kind of tough. We knew we wanted to have it outside so that we could be under the full moon. But finding a safe place where we wouldn't be disturbed was a challenge. We thought of Malibu Beach, but decided that it may be too remote and some weirdo might bother us. The same went for parkland, and as Tri, Zorrita, and I all live in apartments with no balconies, we decided doing it at home was a last resort. In the end, my girlfriend Lisa came to the rescue. She is renovating a house in the Hollywood Hills with a huge rooftop balcony and a view of Los Angeles and the whole sky. This was perfect for us to perform our ritual, blessed by the rays of the full harvest Mabon moon casting its light on the proceedings. Lisa was happy for us to do our ritual there and asked if we could bless the house for her as a part of the ritual. The blessing worked wonders, because not long after, Lisa invited me to move into her beautiful home!

The day of the ritual was a mad dash for me from one esoteric store to the other. First I had to pick up our wolf's heart and its pewter canister from Panpipes. There I also found a perfect Book of Shadows (a huge slab of linen parchment bound between two plates of wood and carved with a pentagram on the front). Also on the shopping list were dragon's blood ink, a porcupine quill for writing in the book, charcoal discs, black candles for the altar, and white tealights in little glass jars to mark out our circle. I knew Zorrita and Tri were out running similar errands buying crystals, mirrors, and shells to bless and empower for our home shrines, more candles, and the blood prickers!

Finally it was time to prepare to leave. I took a long shower and meditated on what we were doing tonight: initiating a coven, a powerful bond between three women that would serve as a magickal temple of learning and experience in this world and all the worlds in between. As the warm water ran down my body, I visualized all the accumulated stress of the day wash away down the drain with it, and I stepped out of the shower feeling fresh and renewed outside and in.

I dressed in black. It was a cool night and over my simple black dress I wore a thick woollen coat and black knee-high boots. I made my eyes up dark and tied my hair back. I was loaded up with bags containing incense, candles, and a large cauldron. The last thing I grabbed before I walked out the door was my camera so I could take photos to commemorate this auspicious event!

As my car drove up the steep drive off Sunset Strip, the garish lights and billboards of the latest blockbuster war movie and anorexic girls dressed in Stella McCartney advertising vodka as a fashion accessory were left behind. I felt like I was entering another world as I wound higher and higher up the hill.

We all arrived simultaneously at the house. It was dark (the electricity wasn't on in the house as it was being renovated), and I fumbled for the keys under the light of a flashlight that Tri held. We didn't say much; we had agreed it would be better not to speak too much before the ritual to preserve a sense of the sacred around the event. We all looked beautiful, though—dark and exotic—ready to make serious magick.

We let ourselves into the house and found our way to the rooftop. The lights of Los Angeles lay at our feet like a carpet of stars. There was a soft, cool breeze and we immediately set about creating a circle of tealights and setting up the altar. We were working within a schedule, as we wanted the dedication to begin at the moment the moon entered her full phase at 8:55. She had not yet risen over the crest of the hill to our left, but her glow cloaking the ridge like an aura showed that her presence in our circle was imminent.

We set up the altar on Zorrita's upturned accordion case. The large black coven candle sat in the center, with the four elements in their corresponding quarters around it: a large red candle in the south for fire; a small cauldron of incense in the east for air; a large spear of quartz crystal for earth in the north; and a bowl of water with salt and a seashell in it in the west for water. My athame was placed in front of me, as I would be using it to cast the circle and consecrate the objects, and there was a bowl of incense I blended especially for the night containing dark herbs sacred to Lilith, our patron goddess: mandrake, mugwort, nightshade, and patchouli. To the side we placed our Book of Shadows, and next to us we each had our home shrine objects: a mirror (Lilith is said to live in mirrors), agate cave crystals (legend has it that Lilith lived in a cave when she left the garden of Eden), and our thumb prickers. I handed the girls copies of the coven creed and invocation of our goddess that we would be reading together.

The moon appeared over the ridge a few minutes before she moved into her full phase, and we quickly made sure all the candles were lit and our preparations done. I cast my eyes around the surrounding houses—all the lights were off, it was quiet, and the breeze had stilled. It seemed like we were very alone. For all I knew, though, people were wondering what these three women—blond, black, and brunette—were doing dressed in black and surrounded by a large ring of candle flame on the roof of their neighbor's house!

We stood around the altar, and I asked the girls if they were ready to commence. They nodded. I raised my arms with my athame pointed high and cast the circle. Having had a practice run in front of the cameras, we already had a good chemistry going and the circle was cast solid and tangible—a fibrillating mass of potential and light encircling us on this dark night. I felt like my athame was capturing strands of moonlight and weaving them together in a mystical web of beauty and light around us.

Once the circle was cast, I lit the coven candle. This thick black candle in its ornate pewter base would now be lit only for our coven meetings when we invoked our patron goddess Lilith.

Together we invoked Lilith, intoning the words that I had written:

Winged goddess of the dawn and night

Bathe us in your dark light.

We Witches gather in your sight

Sharing your eternal flight.

As our three voices blended, in my mind's eye I could see them swirling together like a spiral of incense smoke, forming a passage through which the essence of our goddess Lilith could morph and manifest to join with us in the circle.

The energy amassing within the circle seemed denser, and I felt a little breathless sensing Lilith's presence. I knew the girls felt the same. As one we said our coven creed:

Then and now there is Lilith

Virgin but not celibate

Complete unto herself

All-powerful, all-knowing

All love life and spirit

All dark light and infinite.

The Dark Light of Lilith coven

Is dedicated to magick and wisdom

Power, compassion, and strength

To the rapture of the light

To the ecstasy of the dark.

We then spoke of our individual commitments to the coven, what we personally wanted to achieve and contribute to our coven "in perfect love and perfect trust." We spoke of the importance of respect for each other's space and individual needs within the structure of the group, and I made a point of saying that leadership is created to be shared. As much as I was initiating and leading these early proceedings in the life of our coven, when everyone felt comfortable we would share these tasks equally. We also spoke of the meaning of our covenworld and how important it was for us to perform our daily ritual affirming the existence of and our commitment to the coven, so that it existed not only when we were gathered together physically but also when we were apart. Our covenworld would always be available to us, as it gathered strength and presence in the astral planes. The final part of this ceremony was stating to all the world and all worlds in between that the Dark Light of Lilith coven does now exist.

I had my large cauldron sitting beside me with several glowing discs of charcoal lit within. I sprinkled a large handful of incense, and as the smoke billowed out we passed the various items of our personal shrines through it, consecrating them in the name of the Dark Light of Lilith coven.

The Book of Shadows was the last to be blessed, and I placed it on the altar as we prepared to make our blood offering. I took out the quill and dragon's blood ink and wrote the first initial of my name, and then I pricked my finger and made a print of my blood next to it. The girls then did the same. This was a somber and important moment as we sealed our commitment to our craft and coven with our blood, but there were giggles as we tried to get the thumb prickers to work. In the end we just ended up jabbing ourselves with a pin!

We then cut some hair from each of our heads and, binding the strands together into a knot that looked liked an Egyptian ankh, placed them in the pewter canister containing our wolf's heart. Now we were bound together and empowered with the strength, passion, and cunning of the wolf—our coven totem animal.

With everything blessed and commitments stated, we raised power by chanting a sequence of ancient words that I researched and collated especially for use only by our coven (I will not print them here). The energy was intense, tangible, and delicious, and the sacred sounds spilled from our throats louder and louder, echoing off the hill behind us. As the power peaked, we threw our arms up to sky and screamed, "Lilith, Lilith, Lilith!"

At that very moment, the wind picked up strongly and I felt that our power was swept up and flown to all the corners of the world. After a long moment, we simultaneously placed our hands on the ground to earth our energy. Then I grabbed my camera and we hugged together as I held it out at arm's length and took a photo of the three of us. Our circle was closed but our work was not finished. Our first coven ritual of service was to bless Lisa's house. After we packed up everything on the rooftop, we carried candles through the house and cleansed the space.

An hour and a half after we arrived we were leaving, feeling utterly changed in a profound way. We still hadn't spoken much other than to utter the words of our ritual, but we felt very intimate and close and decided we would head to a coffee shop on Sunset for a snack and a chat. Walking into the softly lit café, our little multicultural group attracted attention. We were black, latino, and white, obviously bonded in an exotic way, our faces flushed with magick. We chatted quietly about the night, sipped our tea, and munched on cookies before departing.

As much as we attempted to ground our energies at the end of the ritual and afterwards by eating together, we all slept restlessly and felt a bit "spooked," particularly Zorrita and me. I wonder if it was because we called on Lilith to be our patron goddess. She has so many mixed legends surrounding her, both very positive and very negative, and maybe we had collected some of the more negative projections of her that others have concocted as we called her into our circle. However, the more we call on her in the circle and carve out our own unique portal for her to manifest through, the purer and more positive her presence will be for us: a bit like pouring water through a carbon-filter purifying jug. We have to purify the way she came to us by forging a stronger grip on what we need her to be and have a more clearly defined and bonded concept of how she should manifest. Apart from that, we three felt absolutely brilliant about the dedication of our coven and agreed that creating such a formal and elaborate ritual was entirely appropriate and necessary to get things off on the right foot.

As you know, I am encouraging you to design and create your own ritual for your coven dedication. Even if you don't have much experience with Witchcraft, with a little bit of time and effort you can create a meaningful and therefore powerful ritual. This may sound scary and intimidating but I promise you it's not impossible, and the rewards you get from doing this yourself, and not just performing something out of a book, will be utterly magickal and worthwhile.

To give you a nudge along, here is a checklist to help you plan this big event!

Setting Up Your Coven

1. Decide on coven members:
   - One or more adept members, out of which one is a leader.
   - At least two other coven members. You need at least three people in a coven for it to be a successful one, as the combined energies and opinions of at least this many people is needed.
2. Decide on ethics and responsibilities, and write a list of these.
3. Pick a patron goddess or god for the coven.
4. Decide on a name for the coven, and choose your coven names if they are going to be different from your everyday names. (My coveners and I decided to keep our everyday names.)

5. Decide on your initial gathering days. It's a good idea in the early stages to agree, for example, that every Thursday night you will meet for coffee and a chat about how the coven is progressing, then that every Sunday night you will do a ritual for the first two months. This will help you build up familiarity and confidence with magickal proceedings. As time goes on, you may agree to only physically meet on esbats (full moon gatherings), special necessary events (like healing rituals and required spellcastings), and sabbats. Of course, though, every morning when you perform your morning dedication (see step 12, page 91), you are psychically meeting with your coven members on the astral planes in your covenworld.

6. Write your coven creed. This should be an evocative piece that states the magickal purpose of the coven and celebrates the patron god/dess in a way that each coven member can personally identify with.

7. Write the invocation of your god/dess. These are the words to be used when invoking their presence in circle.

8. Write your coven's own power-raising chant. As I've mentioned, I researched ancient words and names related to the story of Lilith and concocted a unique chant that only the Dark Light of Lilith coven members know and use.

9. Decide on coven ritual structures and procedures (for example, the methods of casting the circle and performing invocations) so that everyone can learn them. These will be pasted in your Book of Shadows.

10. Home shrines act as a personal doorway to your covenworld. I have two altars at home, one for my general personal magick and one representing my coven membership—it is in front of this altar that I perform my morning dedication. We agreed on certain objects relating to Lilith that our shrines would need to include: a black candle, an agate cave crystal (as I've mentioned, legend says she lived in a cave when she left the Garden of Eden), a small mirror

(again, Lilith is also said to live in mirrors), and an image of an owl—a night bird of wisdom and related to Lilith in her winged aspect. We also agreed that our coven totem, the wolf heart, would initially stay on my shrine but would be shared around equally, staying at each of our homes. When you are deciding what should be included in your home shrines, be guided by what your patron god/dess holds sacred and be as creative as you like.

11. Coven member blessing. I also created a coven member blessing that is standard and can be used from covener to covener as an acknowledgement and blessing within the circle. Ours goes:

> **(Name), I honor you as**
>
> **Witch of the Dark Light of Lilith coven.**
>
> **May you always grow ever stronger**
>
> **And more powerful**
>
> **In heart, mind, spirit, and magick.**

12. Morning dedication. This is an important affirmation of magickal intent. It also works to align the astral and psychic energies of the coveners between the worlds in the sacred space of the covenworld. You can write a dedication together using ours as a guideline, if you like (see sidebar this page).

**Personal
Morning Dedication**

Light your altar candle and incense. Close your eyes, breathe deeply, center and focus within. Meditate on "the green"—the calm, still place that exists within where your spirit dwells outside the realm of everyday experience.

With the index finger of your power hand (the one you write with), perform the Pentagram Salute (like the sign of the cross that Christians use but touching third eye (between eyebrows) then right breast, left shoulder, right shoulder, left breast, third eye again). Then say:

*In perfect love
and perfect trust,
I dedicate myself to the
Universal Forces of Magick
and declare myself Witch
of the (name) coven.*

Coven Dedication Ritual Preparation

1. Choose the location and time of event.

2. Write up the ritual outline and agree on appropriate attire.

3. Make a list of all objects required and go shopping, if necessary. Make the appropriate incense, if you like, and choose your coven totem.

Coven Dedication Ritual

1. Shower/bathe with intent to purify, and dress in ritual attire.

2. Gather at the location.

3. Prepare the altar and, if preferred, physically mark out the circle.

4. Cast the circle.

5. Invoke patron god/dess.

6. State coven creed.

7. Each covener verbally confirms commitment to the coven and discusses the importance of personal supportive coven practice as well as group gatherings to maintain the existence of the covenworld.

8. Bless and consecrate all coven and personal objects of magick (we did this by passing each object through specially blended incense smoke).

9. Write coveners' names and make offering of blood in coven Book of Shadows to seal intent.

10. Empower the coven totem (we did this by cutting and binding our hair together and placing it in the canister with the wolf's heart).

11. Raise power to announce the existence of the coven and to kickstart the covenworld.

12. Ground any energy raised by placing your hands on the ground.

13. Close the circle.

14. Eat together and further ground energy.

15. Go home, have interesting dreams, and wake up as an empowered member of your coven!

Coven Totem

It is not essential to have one, but an object that symbolizes the power of your coven can be empowered and act as a conduit for the coven's unique energy and magick. We chose a wolf's heart, but you could choose just about anything whose symbolism means something to you: an eagle feather, a shark's tooth, a beautiful crystal, an ancient fossil... whatever you like. Keep it in a special container and put something physical from each coven member and any new coven member in there with it (hair is usually the best). In this way, you are bound together and empowered by what the object represents.

Making Magick Together

You may be an absolute champion at meditating and visualizing as a solitary Witch but the results that can be attained by combining your efforts with others will utterly amaze you. Aligning yourselves psychically is an important part of your development as a coven. Psychic connection is also essential in creating a potent covenworld—the projection of your united intent and will that manifests on the astral plane as an entity unto itself. A well-conjured covenworld can work to protect, support, and strengthen you as you go about your daily lives, without needing to consciously "think about it." The only way to achieve a really powerful covenworld is to hone your group skills of meditation and visualization.

Group Meditation

Group meditation can be as simple as sitting in a circle, holding hands and thinking about a color together, or it can be more elaborate, involving certain body positions and whole lists of imagery to contemplate. Following are some very effective yet relatively simple disciplines to learn that will enhance not only your covenworld and your life in general, but also ritual activities like circle-casting, power-raising, and spellcasting, .

Discipline 1

Stand together in a circle with the tips of your fingers of Saturn (the middle fingers) touching the covener's next to you. Synchronize your breathing so that you are gently inhaling and exhaling together. See everyone's conjoined breath blend together in the center and be aware that you are breathing in the air that has been in your covenmates' lungs—you are all intimately connected in this way. You will probably feel a spontaneous cone of power start to whiz through and around you as you are all connected by your Saturn fingers and your breath becomes increasingly charged with your unified intent. Stay in the moment for as long as you can until one person (chosen before the ritual begins) speaks out:

"Now unified as one, our coven's work is done."

Deeply inhale the energy that has built up, open your eyes, and drop your hands to the floor to earth any excess energy. Sit and discuss your thoughts and impressions, writing up anything important in your Book of Shadows.

Discipline 2

I will never forget the experience I had of a group color meditation when I was in high school! We had Friday afternoon electives and I had chosen yoga. We were all invited to lie on our backs in rows, visualize a color, and then picture it moving through our bodies before passing it on to the next person. I sensed green and pink coming to me from the girl next to me, and when we finished I asked her if that's what she'd sent me, and she said yes! Color is not only a potent and familiar thing to psychically project, but it is also healing and balancing. I have varied the following meditation slightly from my own experience to make it more effective for group consciousness-raising.

Lie opposite each other with feet touching sole to sole. This will be easy if you have an evenly numbered coven, but if not have one pair do it for five minutes while the others sit around them doing breath meditation. (Breath meditation basically focuses on inhaling and exhaling. You don't want to interfere with the color meditating pair.) Agree on which person starts, then close your eyes and take some deep breaths together. The agreed-on person then starts to send a color. First they picture it forming like a cloud or a pool of liquid in their head before seeing it floating or streaming down their bodies to run into the other person. The color is sent like this until someone who has been appointed as the timer says "It is done." Then the meditators open their eyes and the person receiving the color describes what color it was they were visualizing. You will find that 90 percent of the time they will be correct, but this success rate will depend on how confident and powerful the meditator is. Then the meditation is reversed, with the other person receiving the color. In an unevenly numbered coven, everyone rotates until all have had a turn.

Discipline 3

Sit together with your arms stretched out to either side with the tips of your Saturn fingers (middle) touching. Together, picture that a presence is supporting your arms. This is not a spirit presence that you are invoking, just a sensation of support. This arm position is difficult to maintain under normal consciousness; however, with the coven psychically linked and visualizing support, it becomes effortless, and you can hold it for five minutes or more. Try it and see! When you understand how combined intent can support and help you bear physical hardship, you will understand how to apply that collective energy to healing spells and rituals that you do for each other and anyone else in need.

Discipline 4

You may like to record these instructions and then play it as a guided group meditation. Lie in a circle with your heads touching and your bodies lying out like the spokes of a wheel. Where your heads are touching, see a sphere of purple/violet light appear and pulse. See this expand, gradually shifting to a shimmering white circle of light that blankets you all. See this wheel of light now start to spin—your bodies are the spokes so you, too, feel yourselves spin in a sunwise direction (counterclockwise in the Southern Hemisphere). Collectively, you may feel as if your bodies lift from the floor, and some of you may have a spontaneous out-of-body experience. Stay in this meditation for at least fifteen minutes. Then (and this is why it's handy to record the instructions) the words "As above, so below; as the universe, so the soul" can be spoken by all or one, and the wheel will gradually slow down. Then the words "Grounded are we in body and spirit—unified, strong, and infinite" can be spoken. This is a signal for everyone to open their eyes. Roll over on your stomachs and rest your heads on the floor to ground any excess energy. Then just relax and discuss your impressions, and write up anything pertinent in your Book of Shadows.

These disciplines will psychically align and link you, and help you develop wills of steel. Following are some activities you can undertake once you have refined your group skills of psychic meditation.

Dream Triggers

This one is good if you are away together on a retreat and sleeping in the same place, or if you have a good couple of days off from work or school, as it involves disturbing your sleep repeatedly throughout the night!

Go to bed with an alarm clock and phone next to your bed. Set the alarm to go off at an agreed-on time, waking you up. Then call each other on the phone (or speak if you are sleeping in the same space), say a specific word (the dream trigger), and then go back to sleep.

Another way to achieve this without calling or speaking to each other is to agree on a list of words, and then read and visualize a word from the list at each alarm call. For example:

You all agree on a list of words: green, ocean, wolf. Next, ascertain that you will all likely be asleep by (for example) 12 midnight, so the first alarm will be set for 1:30 AM, the second at 3:30 AM, and the third at 5 AM. When you wake up with each alarm, say the word out loud ("green"), then visualize the word, set the alarm for the next agreed time, and go back to sleep. Repeat this for the remaining words and alarm times.

Upon waking, immediately write down your dream recollections in a dream diary (a book especially used for dream recall and analysis), and then compare your dreams at the next gathering.

Profound insights can be achieved for ideas for rituals and other coven practices. It is quite likely that you will appear in each other's dreams. Make sure you keep a detailed record. A good way to prepare for this dream trigger work is to each individually keep a dream diary for two weeks before-hand so that you get used to recalling your dreams. Just keep the book and a pen next to your bed, and on awakening write down anything you remember straightaway. It doesn't matter if it seems like gobbledy-gook, just capture whatever recollections you have. When you analyze it later, you will see patterns appear—and undoubtedly some revelations that come with the recognition of these patterns!

Astral Traveling

When I was in my late teens, I had a problem with compulsive eating. This might have been because I worked in a health-food store for a time, and one of my jobs was to pack the snacks into individual bags. Carob-coated almonds, apricot bars, roasted salted cashews . . . I couldn't stop stuffing myself. This crossed over into all other areas of my life, and I was binge eating all the time, taking handfuls of senna tablets (an herbal laxative) at night to crap it all out in the morning. How gross—and very unhealthy for my body and my spirit. I decided to undertake a course of hypnotherapy to see if it would help, so once a week for six weeks I saw a woman who would relax me to a state where I could recall the various reasons in my life's journey that triggered me to behave in this self-destructive way. Thanks to this process, I was able to stop the overeating and laxative abuse—plus I got a nice bonus: all the hypnotherapy switched on my ability to travel out of my body. I began to astral travel regularly, with very little effort.

Astral traveling is where a person's spirit leaves their body and either travels through the physical world that the body is inhabiting or shifts between the realms and travels in other realities.

My personal experience was that I would begin by meditating on nothing or nothingness. This is what my hypnotist prescribed for me to do for twenty minutes morning and night during the treatment. "Nothing" or "nothingness" is a black, silent, emotionless state of zero. But from nothing comes something: as I hovered in the absolute nil of the moment, I would also be contemplating the fecund potential of this state. When I fully grasped this, I would get an intense pressure in my third eye area (between my eyebrows) and then feel myself "lift"—in some ways it was more like movement outwards in every direction; not so much elevating, but expanding beyond my skin. The recollections I had immediately after my astral travels were not so much a stream of connected images but feelings that in one minute I would be in the room next door, the next out on the street, and so on. As I did it more often, I would really make an effort to notice details of my surroundings and then go back and check the next day in my waking hours to see if my recollections were correct. Quite a few times the tangible memories I had, like a freshly bloomed red flower in a garden next door, or a new band flyer stuck to a pole down the street, were indeed correct.

The more abstract qualities of my traveling between the worlds had more to do with colors, light or the absence of it, and—funnily enough—sensory events: a smoky smell and a metallic taste in the back of my throat. I wrote the recollections of these astral journeys in my Book of Shadows, and the recurring theme of my travels was that they were insights into the nature of existence and spirit as permeating all things and time being an illusion—like the song lyric I once wrote: "linear time—it's a wonderful lie."

To astral travel as a coven and attempt to meet outside of your bodies, here is an exercise you may find helpful. Choose a location that you all agree on. Place a physical representation of yourselves there to help draw your spirits: some hair from each of you entwined and placed in a container with a clear quartz crystal and buried or hidden in the spot that you decide to meet in is a good way of ensuring you all navigate your way successfully there. You could perhaps all decide that you are going to meditate at exactly 11 PM and "meet" at the park a few blocks away, where your homing signal is buried. Then perform the following ritual at an agreed-on time.

A Ritual for Astral Traveling: (Note: This ritual is for those who are seeking to develop the skill of astral traveling. Those who can do it spontaneously can skip these instructions and just get straight to it!)

Burn some incense of nutmeg, or if you can't get this as incense buy it as an essential oil and drop about five drops on water in an oil burner. Nutmeg will assist your consciousness to leave your body. Sit comfortably upright (don't lie down—you'll probably fall asleep!), with your back resting against a wall, your legs straight out in front of you, and your palms in your lap. Breathe deeply and let your body feel heavy like lead. If any thoughts enter your mind, acknowledge them and then visualize them floating away: in and out they come and go, like your breath, in and out, in and out.

Now take your awareness to your third eye (between your eyebrows) and see a spark of light there. See everything around it grow dark as that spark becomes the concentrated essence of you. You are that spark: see your spirit body take shape and form from the spark. When it is glowing very bright, see it leap out of your forehead and hover in the air.

Now, look back at your physical body resting upright against the wall. In your spirit form, start to travel to the agreed meeting location. You may find that this feels like you are "imagining" walking out your front door and down the street. Imagining is fine, because it is the integral step to actually doing it. The shift from you imagining to you astral traveling is very subtle, and you may not even realize it has occurred.

When you "arrive" at the agreed meeting place, look around and see who else is there. For the first few times, don't attempt to communicate by normal physical methods, just relax and see what happens. After a couple of "meetings" like this, you will find that conversations and activities will start to flow—in fact, all sorts of things will start to happen!

When you feel it is time, return back to your body the same way you left it. You might find that you spontaneously appear in front of it rather than walking back, like the way you left. The main thing is that when you see your body in front of you, shrink yourself back to the spark of light and enter back through the third eye of your physical body.

Stay resting there for a moment and really experience the sensation of being back in your physical body. Wiggle your fingers and your toes, stretch a little, and slowly open your eyes. Give yourself a massage; rub your arms and legs, belly, back, and head to awaken your physical self. Then write all your recollections down and compare them to your covenmates'.

The first few times you may feel you are controlling the journey by imagining every step of it, but this will change and one day you will find there is a lot of stuff going on that you are not initiating. The important thing when this happens is to have the ritual of returning to your body highly familiarized so that you can always get back, no matter what.

Sometimes having a keyword can be a good idea. If you are surfing the astral planes and you don't like where you are, you can state the keyword and it will immediately bring you back to standing in front of your body. Sometimes when I have astral traveled I have seen a silvery cord of light floating from me (like a leg rope!), and I know that this cord attaches me to my physical self. But it is not always there and that's why I think a keyword is a very good thing to have as a backup to always find your way home. Up until recently I used the keyword "present." I have changed it now and will keep it private—as it is best you keep yours, even from your other coven members. To set a keyword, go into the meditation as described above but when you have the spark of self ignited in your third eye, instead of casting it forward to leave your body, keep your awareness focused within your third eye. Now say the word at least twenty times, either out loud or silently. As you do this, fully comprehend that this word is the key that transcends all boundaries and will immediately make your physical body accessible to your spirit, no matter what. By the way, the keyword can be as elaborate as you like—it can even be a word you make up. The only requisite is that it is only known to you.

Astral traveling gets easier the more you do it, and when you share the experience as part of a coven ritual the tangibility and clarity of the experience will be enhanced. Of course, you can go on as many solo journeys as you like, too. Keep a record of what you experience and any insights gained, as these will be valuable tools to assist you in the development of your craft.

Coven Dedications

As I have suggested in an earlier chapter, you will be performing your coven dedications every morning, but you can also do it at other times during the day, synchronized with each other. For example, agree to do the dedications every hour from 5 to 11 PM for one week. At the precise, agreed moment of the hour, spend two minutes performing the dedication and thinking of your coven members. Repeated affirmations of your connection with each other will create powerful psychic links.

Group Spells

There are so many books on spellcasting, both solitary and in groups, that it is truly redundant to list more here. What I want to suggest instead is that you and your coven members become very good at "charging" objects. Charging is basically you projecting your combined, focused will to empower an object, person, or even event.

Charging Ritual

Cast a circle as usual. Place the object to be empowered in the center of the circle, either on the altar, on a table, or wherever—just make sure it is in the center and can be seen and focused on by everyone. For example, it can be your combined coven jewelry, a person who needs healing (they don't need to be there physically—you can have a photo too), or a written description of an upcoming event that you want to bless.

All together, touch your fingers of Saturn (the middle finger) with the next person's, and breathe in unison. Whoever is the leader then says the following:

For the good of all, with harm to none,

Our power is great, our work's begun.

All visualize a beam of light leaving your individual third eye chakras and see them fuse together as a ball of light around what is being charged. You will likely feel tingles all over, as you not only power up the object but power up each other. When it is obvious the power is peaking, the leader says:

For the good of all, with harm to none,

Our power is great, our work is done.

On "done," everyone exhales together and says:

So mote it be.

This seals the charge, and the object, person, or event is empowered. Next, it is a good idea for the coveners to place their hands on the floor and earth any excess power. The charging ritual can then be completed by opening the circle as normal.

Witch Tip

I think the key to understanding and honoring the sabbats as a coven is to consider them celebratory events—even the more somber ones like Samhain and Mabon. A way to effectively do this can be to link up with other covens to share the event or to attend festivals honoring the event.

The Sabbats

The sabbats are Witchcraft's holy days like Christmas is to Christians and Hanukkah is to Jews. There are eight of them spaced roughly six weeks apart throughout the year and they correspond to agricultural and astronomical events. The cycle of these sabbats is known as the wheel of the year: when we "turn" the wheel, we honor and respect the cycles of destruction, death, and decay, and birth, growth, and renewal as we see them spin in the worlds of matter and spirit. In an age of supermarkets and refrigerators, where we can consume food out of its natural season, the homage to these festivals of old keeps us in touch with the energies of the earth and our naturalness today.

I have written at length about the sabbats and how to celebrate them in my previous books *Witch: A Magickal Journey* and *Witchin': A Handbook for Teen Witches*, plus there are numerous books on the subject written by other authors as recommended at the back of this book. However, I have broken them down here as accessible points of reference on the following pages, and I encourage you to further research each sabbat by reading books, surfing the 'net, and speaking to other Witches about how to celebrate these sacred events.

As the sabbats are seasonal, in the Northern Hemisphere they are opposite to the Southern Hemisphere. The greater sabbats are the four agricultural events: Samhain, Imbolc, Beltane, and Lammas. They are centered around the Pagan cycles of agriculture as experienced by the Northern European tribes and have been reawakened within the modern Wiccan tradition. The four lesser sabbats are the solstices and equinoxes.

Samhain

Date: October 31 (Northern Hemisphere), May 1 (Southern Hemisphere).

Land: The final storing of food for winter, a clear indication that winter is coming.

Life: The ending and the beginning—a Festival of Death is celebrated. It is a time where the veils shrouding spirit from matter lift and those departed from the physical world can be invited to join those they left behind.

Altar items: Black candles, apples and pomegranates, carved pumpkins.

Ritual theme: Honoring and contacting the spirits of departed loved ones.

Coven activity: Visit a cemetery together and have a picnic.

Yule/Winter Solstice

Date: December 20–23 (Northern Hemisphere), June 20–23 (Southern Hemisphere)—check a reliable astronomical calendar for exact date.

Land: The longest night before the sun is born anew and begins its ascent to summer.

Life: A Witch's Christmas and a time to burn the Yule log (slow-burning wood) and honor the belief that from death comes life.

Altar items: Gold candles, mistletoe, pine cones.

Ritual theme: Celebrate friendship, companionship, and abundance.

Coven activity: Enjoy a big, hearty feast of casseroles, puddings, mead, and mulled wine, and exchange presents. Stay up all night lighting candles to welcome the dawning of the new sun.

Imbolc

Date: February 1 (Northern Hemisphere), August 1 (Southern Hemisphere).

Land: New life awakens, buds appear on trees and plants, and animals start to mate.

Life: Cleanse your emotions by releasing old grudges and hang-ups; awaken the creative spirit by embarking on a new hobby like playing an instrument or making jewelry.

Altar items: A corn dolly (representing Brigid, the sacred goddess of this time) surrounded by white candles and red blossoms.

Ritual theme: Purification, transformation, and new beginnings, a sacred time for women and the arts; the promise of spring means the awakening of the Maiden (so recharge some girl power!). Cleansing and purifying, her warming breath heals the land and our hearts of the winter cold, and promises new energies and approaching abundance.

Coven activity: A big spring cleanout—help each other and hold a shared garage sale the following week. Finish the day with an evening of poetry reading and wine.

Ostara/Spring Equinox

Date: March 20–23 (Northern Hemisphere), September 20–23 (Southern Hemisphere).

Land: Day and night stand equal; spring has arrived, plants are flowering, and animals birthing.

Life: A time to honor the young God and the positive balance between men and women.

Altar items: Green and yellow candles, eggs.

Ritual theme: Plant your future! Gather together and plan a new flowerbed (either outside or in pots) of sweetly scented buds and herbs. As you sow the seeds, chant a charm for good fortune: "New life we bring forth from the earth: in our hearts, homes, and minds, we are blessed by the divine."

Coven activity: Have a chocolate egg hunt!

Beltane

Date: May 1 (Northern Hemisphere), October 31 (Southern Hemisphere).

Land: A time of passion and sensuality. In times of old, people made love in the fields to ensure the fertility of the upcoming year's crops.

Life: Honor the fertility of your life.

Altar items: Red and white ribbons and candles.

Ritual theme: The Maypole dance is the traditional celebration of this event. Dress in red and white, burn lavender in a fire, and jump over it to ensure the fertility of body, mind, and spirit in the coming year.

Coven activity: Have a sensual feast with your partners attending, and make love under the stars after.

Litha/Summer Solstice

Date: June 20–23 (Northern Hemisphere), December 20–23 (Southern Hemisphere)—check a reliable astronomical calendar for exact date.

Land: The longest day of the year with the sun at its peak of power—from this day on, it will begin the descent to the dark of winter.

Life: Celebrate all that is abundant in life but temper that joy with a solemn respect for endings; for as sure as everything comes, everything also goes.

Altar items: Sunflowers, cauldron with hot coals inside and incense of myrrh and frankincense.

Ritual theme: Do a divination by gazing at the patterns formed by the hot coals in your cauldron.

Coven activity: Any fun activity together under the heat of the noonday sun—perhaps a game of cricket or volleyball on the beach.

Lammas

Date: August 1 (Northern Hemisphere), February 1 (Southern Hemisphere).

Land: The first harvest; food is put away for winter. The days are still long and hot, but the dark is approaching. The traditional food to eat at this time is bread and corn.

Life: A time to honor the rewards of hard labor and the results of plans and goals made in the previous year that have come to fruition.

Altar items: Corn, dried plants and fruits.

Ritual theme: Bury any attitudes or habits that no longer serve you by writing them down, wrapping them around a stone, and burying them deep in the earth.

Coven activity: Bake bread and eat together, affirming that the positive application of skills of body, will, and spirit always bring desired results.

Mabon/Autumn Equinox

Date: September 20–23 (Northern Hemisphere), March 20–23 (Southern Hemisphere)—check a reliable astronomical calendar for exact date.

Land: Day and night stand equal as the second harvest is stored.

Life: A time to reflect on the coming rest and respite of winter.

Altar items: Autumn leaves, brown and orange candles, dried flowers, wood and bracken.

Ritual theme: Meditate together on death by lying together on the ground in "corpse pose" (flat on back with hands down to the side), radiating out in a circle with heads touching.

Coven activity: Watch the sun set together.

I recommend you concoct and choreograph your own celebrations of the sabbats as much as possible. There is no one book that has the "correct" and "approved" words for any Witchcraft ritual—including mine! You are welcome to memorize elaborate scripts and reenact the myth of the wheel of the year that you will find in many books, but if someone else has written the words and actions, they could be missing an essential ingredient to make them truly honoring of the earth and empowered; that ingredient is your personal contribution. Any activity undertaken by rote will not churn up the ancient energies that the sabbat celebrations can be conduits for. For maximum results, keep interested and engaged in what you do.

It is important to really make an effort to meet for the sabbats, at the very least the four greater ones. However, sometimes it's just not possible. Last Samhain I was very busy doing media appearances (Halloween is a public Witch's busiest time of the year!), so I sent this email to my coven mates and we performed this ritual at our own homes.

> Hi girls,
> As you are aware, I cannot meet for the sabbat tonight. I feel, however, I am doing something constructive and appropriate in being out there speaking of the real Witches' meaning of Halloween/Samhain. I would like to suggest that we all individually meditate on the significance of this sacred time by performing this ritual. At our Lilith shrines, perform the following dedication:

KISS

When I started out, the rituals I created were very basic and the words I used very simple. Now after nineteen years I can forge far more elaborate undertakings and still stay engaged and potently in the moment, fueling my actions with passionate intent. So as I've mentioned before, Keep It Simple Sorceress/er, until you are adept and familiar with the themes and messages of the sabbats. Most importantly, remember that the sabbats are a time of collectively rejoicing in our lives as Witches.

Do the Pentagram Salute three times for blessing (as in the Morning Dedication (page 91)), then speak the following words:

On this holy night of the darkest sabbat,
I honor those who have gone before and after
Between the worlds, all time is now
And all sorrow is laughter.

I rejoice in the cycles of Death and Life
And draw strength and solace in the knowledge
That as we live we also shall die.

I revel in the mysterious beauty of life and death
And understand that as everything begins, so must it end.

I see this as a blessing and gift and choose to live
In the moment of eternal bliss.

Next, meditate on the meaning of these words, and then say the names of all the deceased that you choose to honor and acknowledge on this holy night. Then, in honor of Lilith, chant our sacred chant, offering the energy you raise to the memory of those departed.

Blessed be.

In closing this chapter, I want to encourage you all to be bold and spontaneous in your work together as a coven. Try not to be worried about doing things "wrong" and get nervous, hesitant, and self-conscious when working magick as a group.

Remember . . .

+ There are no mistakes in Witchcraft, only lessons.

+ Obstacles are opportunities for positive change and growth.

+ Be patient and persevere: anything worthwhile takes effort.

+ Experiment, explore, and enjoy!

Goddess Gatherings

Magickal gatherings don't necessarily have to be intense coven gatherings of Wiccan initiates to raise power. Events like Goddess Gatherings are a great way to mix socializing and magick and to let non-Wiccan friends share our enchanted lifestyles! I have a lot of fun organizing Goddess Gatherings. A gathering is pretty much a dinner party for goddesses—only with a ritual and some spellcasting thrown in!

Anyone can attend: the only prerequisite (other than being a chick—although, of course, blokes can have their own God Gatherings) is an open heart and an open mind.

It's lovely, because people who are not sure about being full-blown Witches can experience some magick-making in a safe and fun environment. Even if there is only one Witch who is really adept (or even just a few beginners), it is amazing how much positive energy can be conjured and the kind of transformation that can be initiated when like-minded people gather together.

My Hollywood Goddess Gatherings came about when my good girlfriend Coral and I were chatting one afternoon. She is a brilliant garden designer with an amazing appreciation of beauty in nature and is very in tune with the earth, the seasons, and the phases of the moon. We were discussing how a full moon was coming up in a couple of weeks and that it happened to fall on the Witches' sacred sabbat of Mabon—the Autumn Equinox, when day and night stand equal.

We both agreed it would be nice to have a girls-only dinner party under the full moon at Coral's lovely home in the Topanga Canyon above Malibu. It would be a good way to catch up with acquaintances and make some new friends. Then we agreed to take it one step further: we decided to have a Goddess Gathering, and, as I explained to Coral, use the auspicious time of a full moon on the equinox to empower us and bring around any desired transformation and change in our lives.

The plan was for the (mortal!) goddesses to arrive at 8 PM, conduct the ritual at 8:30 PM, and then eat, drink, and be merry until the witching hour!

The first step was to invite the goddesses. Most of Coral's friends didn't know much about Witchcraft but were open to new experiences and loved the exotic sound of a gathering. I also needed to create an outline for the ritual we would be doing, so we could let everyone know what they needed to bring. I decided to keep it fairly simple, with the main focus being transformation and having great desires realized.

Coral and I sent out emails to the goddesses in our lives:

Goddesses!

It is time to gather under a full moon to bewitch and share good cheer.

A night of empowerment and enchantment awaits; be at Coral's at the stroke of eight!

Our full moon magick starts at 8:30 PM with a spellbinding supper afterwards.

Come dressed opulently in lush pinks and reds like the luscious goddesses you are! Bring with you on a piece of paper a list of your deepest desires, for this is the night that your dreams come true!

The next step was to create an appropriate menu. I explained to Coral that Mabon is a festival of the harvest—in the distant past, it was this part of the year that food would be stored away for the coming cold and dark of winter. In the world of magick, it is a time to acknowledge the rewards of our hard labor and rest secure in the knowledge that the universe always provides if we accept it.

Partnered with the conjuring power of a full moon, our menu needed to feature foods of the harvest: dried fruits, nuts, root vegetables, and grains. We also needed food and beverage to honor the Goddess: apples for love, berries for abundance, and sweet mead, fine champagne, and sparkling grape juice (for the non-drinkers like me) as libations to her.

Now, Coral and I can cook, but we're certainly not the long-lost sisters of Martha Stewart! For this special night, we brought in some help from Coral's neighbor, Nancy, who is a brilliant cook. She loved the idea of a "magickal menu," and together we created our feast:

Full Moon Goddess Gathering Menu

Everything on this menu is created with magick in mind!

Entrée

Dried fruits and nuts: symbolic of the successful harvest experienced on the land and in our lives.

Brie and strawberries: passionate and romantic, these foods are sacred to love.

Main

Moroccan vegetable stew with couscous/brown rice: this rich and hearty stew celebrates the harvest and blesses our endeavors.

Breads: sacred to the harvest, they remind us that trusting in our dreams and desires and honoring our efforts and experiences guarantees a unique and richly rewarding life.

Dessert

Blackberry and apple tart: berries are the fruits of passion, and apples are sacred to Aphrodite.

Libations

Moët & Chandon: a heavenly beverage!

Sparkling grape juice: for abundance.

Honey mead: to toast the moon during our ritual.

Witch Tip

Remember:
It is your comprehension
of the world around you
that allows it to manifest
and speak to you in
an enchanted way.
Look for magick and
it will make itself
known to you.

When you are planning the menu, research the magickal meanings of foods using books and the Internet, but don't be afraid to use your intuition and imagination too. For example, if berries are in season and looking lush, ripe, and sweet, and you have decided your ritual will be for fertility, then they will be perfect, as they obviously evoke an appreciation of the qualities of fertility.

On the night, I arrived early at Coral's and she had already made everything look lovely. The dining table was outside and decorated with white and pink flowers, fairy lights and shimmering glitter; overhead, hanging from a tree, was a candelabra lit with small, scented candles.

A little distance away behind some trees was a circular stone table and benches. I set about transforming the setting from a picnic area into a mystical grove. First I set up symbols of the four elements on the table. (Please note these correspondences are for the Northern Hemisphere—for the Southern Hemisphere, you would need to put fire in the north and earth in the south, but leave air in the east and water in the west.)

In the north quarter I placed a big piece of quartz crystal for the earth element. In the east, I placed a clay dish filled with heat-absorbing sand and charcoal discs to burn incense on for the element of air. On this night I had made a beautiful blend of resins of myrrh and copal infused with essential oils of jasmine and neroli.

In the south, I set up a big, white jasmine-scented candle for the fire element. In the west, I placed a crystal bowl of water with a seashell in it and a pinch of salt to make a mini-ocean.

In the center of what was now our altar, I placed a large cast-iron cauldron and an altar candle. I set out twelve glasses (we would be toasting the moon and pouring libations to the Goddess), and alongside these I placed twelve little, red, rose-scented candles for love. Next to the cauldron, I set a vase in which were twelve long-stemmed roses. I scattered tealight candles in glass jars in the surrounding plants and trees, and the whole area looked liked a fairy grove, potent and ready to make magick in.

By this time the goddesses had started to arrive. Everyone was laughing and smiling and looking divine. The dress code of opulent and Goddesslike was definitely honored! When everyone was assembled, I gave a little speech about what we would be doing: a ritual to honor our efforts over the past year, and then we would invoke our new dreams into reality. I asked everyone if they had their list of what they wished to bring into their lives in the coming year; two people realized they'd left theirs at home and there was a mad scramble to find paper and pens! But soon after, we were walking single file toward our altar.

I was so impressed with the way everyone embraced the proceedings. I was really the only Witch there who was familiar with what we were doing, but every "goddess" had at some point in her life been in a church or perhaps on a spiritual retreat and could relate to the sacred and serious nature of what we were doing together.

We gathered in a circle around the table, eyes bright and full of expectancy. I talked through the details of what we would be doing. It's important to familiarize everyone with the general ritual outline so you can all relax and focus on the feeling of being in the space and not worrying about having to remember things and what comes next.

Full Moon Goddess Gathering Ritual

I started by chanting my favorite Sanskrit chant. It is very euphoric and always unites everyone's energy psychically and emotionally. Then I sprinkled some incense on the burning discs, and as the air filled with an entrancing scent, I cast a circle by formally acknowledging our sacred space and invoking the elements.

Then it came time to declare the Goddess present as a part of the circlecasting ritual. I asked everyone, in turn, to take a rose from the vase and pass it to the woman to her left, bestowing a kiss on each cheek and saying, "(Name), thou art goddess." This was a beautiful moment, as some of us were strangers, but in this moment we were all intimate, united as goddesses. A warm feeling of love and acceptance filled our circle so strongly that it brought tears to my eyes.

We then joined hands as I declared:

Tonight we sisters gather under a full and harvest moon

On this sacred night of the equinox.

We honor what we have and what we yet have not

We celebrate our challenges and rewards of successful schemes

And on the wings of magick, we fly toward our dreams.

Then, one at a time, we each lit our little red love candle from the large altar candle flame and then read our wishes out loud. As accompaniment at first I alone sang the Wiccan Goddess Chant, "Isis, Astarte, Diana, Hecate, Demeter, Kali, Inanna," but it didn't take long before the other goddesses joined in. When her list was read, each goddess threw it into the cauldron along with a sprinkled pinch of incense, fanning the spirals of smoke to the sky, carrying her wishes with it.

After the final list was read, we all joined hands and really started chanting to raise power. As our voices grew in intensity, tingles went up my spine and I could tangibly feel our cone of power extending into the heavens. All the animals around us could sense it too, because all of a sudden dogs started howling, birds started calling, and crickets began chirping. All of nature was joining us in intent and desire. It was truly amazing! At the peak of the cone, we ceased together intuitively and I called out:

By one, this spell is done

By two, it shall come true

By three, so must it be

By four, for the good of all

By five, our dreams come alive!

Then we all clapped our hands once in unison and quickly rested them on the ground to let the energy drain out. We were all silent for a moment and then, all of a sudden, there was an eruption of voices: "Wow!", "That was amazing!", "I could really feel that!" We had certainly cast a powerful spell together.

We raised a glass of mead each, toasting "To the Goddess, to us!" and then poured a little on the ground as libations to her and to ourselves.

Then it was time for our feast. Coral and I had both decided to play witchy dinner music, which in our taste amounted to Kate Bush, The Mediæval Bæbes, Australian enchantress Wendy Rule, and ambient trance music. Soon Kate was serenading us as our own voices rose in shared discussion.

Our dinner conversation was not the usual fare—it was deep and thoughtful, hilarious and revealing. United, we drew strength from each other's sharing of experiences, triumphs, and tragedies. As the evening finally drew to a close after midnight, I reminded the goddesses not to speak of what had transpired on this night: spells that are cast are best served with silent respect, trusting them to whisk away and do their business. Gossiping and constantly going over the events would be like planting a seed and then digging it up to see how it's going.

We left the gathering changed—invigorated and renewed.

As I was putting away my ritual tools and preparing for the trip home, I reflected on the night and was really touched—what brave, special creatures the women of this night were, ready to leap off the precipice of fear, cynicism, and doubt into the arms of trust, wisdom, and empowerment!

I'm sure you're dying to know . . . did the spells work? I can tell you mine certainly did! I don't often do spells for myself—at this point in my magickal evolution it is more appropriate for me to serve and assist others—but on this night I needed a shift and some clarity in a situation relating to someone who seemed to care for me but was constantly sending mixed signals. Within a day of doing the spell, all of a sudden that person was very clear with their intentions. The shift in their attitude was so remarkable I could only put it down to the spell. I then had to decide if I wanted to return this person's clear intentions. (Once I knew what was going on, I actually decided it would be better not to.)

The other goddesses all experienced results, ranging from job promotions to love restored to being confronted with the very difficulties they sought to avoid (but instead of being thwarted by them, they had the energy to blast through the problem and resolve the issue that was blocking them from happiness).

The wonderful thing about creating something like a Goddess Gathering is not just the results of the spells cast. You realize that, when joined with others in a magickal mindset, your whole life is a work of magick, an expression of your unique creative essence. When you experience the divine and mystical in a tangible way, initiated by your efforts rather than, for example, that of a priest at the front of a church, you are empowered as a whole being, spiritually, emotionally, physically, and mentally.

The more Goddess Gatherings and other magickal moments you create in your life, the more wonderful life becomes.

Here is a checklist to help you plan your own gathering.

Goddess Gathering Checklist

1. Decide on an auspicious date.

2. Write an appropriately charmed invitation.

3. Email or post it out to fellow goddesses.

4. Plan the ritual. Do some research and write up the intent, the process, and the incantations. Decide what input each individual goddess should make.

5. Decide what props are needed for the ritual, and organize their availability. For example, candles, feathers, flowers, shells, incense, cauldron, etc.

6. Plan the magickal menu. Again, do research and choose foods that relate to your magickal event and goals. The book *Cunningham's Encyclopedia of Wicca in the Kitchen* by Scott Cunningham has wonderful food correspondences and menu ideas. And while you are deciding on food, you may like to also decide on the music, which will add an extra dimension to the evening's entrancement.

7. Once the RSVPs start flooding in, send out another email informing each goddess of what she will personally need to provide for the gathering. For example, her wish list for the spell, an object she would like blessed, etc.

8. Shopping and cooking. Do as much cooking as you can in advance of the day. You need to be feeling relaxed and ready to make magick on the night, not absolutely trashed from a hell day in the kitchen!

9. Perhaps plan a gift for each of the goddesses. After our gathering, everyone left with the rose they were given and the candle they lit.

10. Type up the goddess menu and a clear outline of the ritual in large, bold print that you can keep on hand to help guide you throughout the proceedings. Having said this, though, it's important that you try to memorize everything, so the proceedings can go smoothly and have maximum magickal effect.

11. The day before, rehearse your ritual and memorize the words you need to.

12. On the day, relax and go with the flow; let spontaneous things happen, but as much as possible stick to the planned ritual so that the power raised is focused for good and maximum effect.

13. Delegate any chores you can so that you don't have so much on your plate that you can't be a goddess on the night!

A tip: The trick to guaranteeing a special and successful ritual is careful planning and practice. This means running through the proceedings in your mind before the event and learning all the invocations and incantations by heart.

When you are actually doing the ritual, people can repeat after the person who leads, but at least one person needs to be very familiar with what is going on.

Good Occasions for a Goddess Gathering

Full moons and new moons are always a good excuse, as are solstices, equinoxes, and sabbats. Also, gatherings don't only have to be at night: dawn, midday, sunset, and twilight are all special, evocative, and atmospheric times.

Birthdays, anniversaries, and other events such as these are generally not a good idea, as they focus too much on an in-

Witch Tip

It is better that no one drinks too much before the ritual. One glass of wine is fine, but if everyone is sloshed there will be more giggling than granting of wishes.

dividual and not enough on the collective. The key to a successful Goddess Gathering, where both magick and merriment are invoked, is a unified purpose and egoless state in each individual.

What About a God Gathering?

Sure, you can have a God Gathering. Pretty much the same instructions apply!

Share the Love

As much as I am part of a coven, I also love to hold open gatherings where people who are not full-time Witches can enjoy some magick. I focus on gatherings for women because I find that in a sacred space surrounded by my sisters I can feel fully empowered in an unencumbered way. This may have something to do with living in Los Angeles, of course, where, unfortunately, good guys are few and far between—dealing with so many male fruit loops in my work means I am less likely to seek out their company in my personal time—and especially my magick-making time!

So share the love and invite your girlfriends to regular communal celebrations of witchery. Birthday parties, dinner parties, and even bachelorette parties can be reinvented as opportunities to empower each other and learn from each other. Together you can become more than the sum of your parts, and the positive energy generated will be a powerful magnet that will attract better life experiences consistently for you all. Too much love is not enough, I always say, and so I like to focus my informal gatherings around conjuring and enhancing more of this energy, as the following rituals and activities demonstrate. They are also perfect to experience as closed coven events, being fun and informal ways to strengthen your covenworld bond.

The following ritual I created for a girlfriend who was going through a tough time in her love life—she too was feeling challenged by the sexual minefield that you encounter every day living in Hollywood as you try to open yourself to love—and needed some nurturing. This ritual can be adapted for any open gathering where you want to honor a girlfriend as a goddess.

The Divine Maiden Ritual of Love and Celebration

Surprise your girlfriend by planning this secretly. Invite her over for movies and pizza, and when she arrives have all her magickal sisters (guests) assembled, your home lit with candles, and the ritual space prepared. If you want to splurge a little, buy her something lovely and white—perhaps a dress or flowing skirt, a cute singlet, and a wrap, and invite her to get changed, as she is to be honored as the Divine Maiden.

Set up your ritual space with the following:

- A low, flat table with a lovely chair (the throne) at one end.

- Pillows and throws scattered around the table (now the altar) for the sisters to comfortably lounge on.

Prior to the ritual you will have declared someone to be the priestess, who will lead the ritual. On the altar, have:

- Pink and red candles for love, sweetly scented with vanilla, strawberry, ylang ylang, and other sensual aromatic oils.

- Bowls of fresh rose petals.

- Fresh flowers: blooms of gardenias, jasmine, white lilies, and peonies are wonderful, but any pretty, scented flowers will be perfect.

- Incense of white sandalwood, jasmine, orange blossom, or similar. You are creating a sacred smoke of luscious, sensual, perfumed energy, so choose something that invokes these qualities.

- The Aphrodite goddess headdress. This can be purchased from any good flower store. Have them make a flowered ring of soft willow branches entwined with blossoms of pale pink (for love) and sprays of small white blooms (to represent sea foam, as Aphrodite rose from the sea on a pale pink shell). You could add little scallop seashells to the headdress to further empower it with Aphrodite's energy.

If budget doesn't allow for a purchased crown, make it yourself. Sweetly scented flowers bound to ribbon and tied atop the Divine Maiden's hair will work perfectly.

Invite the friends to wear magickally chic white clothing and bring champagne and sweet treats (sacred to the Maiden Goddess) for the feasting and libations after the bewitching blessing.

When your Divine Maiden arrives and is over the shock of such a lovely surprise and ready to enter the sacred space, the person designated as priestess can lead her to her throne. All her beloved friends gather in a circle around the altar, which is strewn with the fresh flowers and candles.

In front of the throne rests the sacred crown of Aphrodite, and as the priestess places it on the Maiden's head, she explains that the flowers, vines, and shells are sacred to Aphrodite:

She is now a goddess crowned in Aphrodite's honor—
the patron goddess of the Maiden, sweet sister of divine love
and everlasting beauty of the soul, blessed by the sun, the moon, and the stars.

When everyone is settled, the priestess creates a sacred circle of protection and pure potential, guiding all within to align themselves with the elements of air, earth, fire, and water with the following words:

Tonight we gather in a sacred circle
Vibrant and potent,
Ripe with our dreams and desires.

The priestess then says:

I now honor the four sacred energies,
air, fire, water, and earth.

She invites everyone to focus on breathing together as she says:

Air inspires our dreams
and lifts our spirits.

She then has everyone place their hands over their hearts to feel the warmth of their centers and says:

Fire fuels our goals
and brings positive change.

Then everyone places their open palms on their knees, demonstrating they are ready to receive blessings, and she says:

Water fills our hearts
and nourishes our potential.

Finally, she invites everyone to place their feet firmly on the ground as she says:

Earth anchors our magickal efforts
in the physical realm.

Witch Tip

The Divine Maiden ritual is quite elaborate and wordy—don't let this put you off doing it! If you can memorize the words, fantastic, but it is perfectly okay for the priestess to have cards written with the different invocations in front of her and refer to them during the ritual. As long as everyone else gathered is focused on creating positive, empowered energy, the priestess can concentrate solely on leading the ceremony!

The priestess then honors the Divine Maiden by placing Aphrodite's crown upon her head and saying:

In the name of Aphrodite

We honor thee, (Name)

Maiden sweet and beautiful

Pure and full of love's potential

Thou art blessed on this night

And for evermore.

The priestess then calls everyone to walk forward, two at a time, showering the Divine Maiden with rose petals and affirming:

(Name), thou art blessed by love.

When everyone has showered the Maiden in petals, they hold hands and simply breathe together, focusing on the wonderful energy that is being shared in this timeless moment. When all are aligned in a state of bliss, the priestess asks everyone to again focus on their desire for (Name) to be happy and blessed in love. She then states the Spell Seal of Security:

By one, this spell is done

By two, it shall come true

By three, so must it be

By four, for the good of all

By five, our dreams come alive!

All gathered pass around the Divine Kiss (kissing each other from cheek to cheek), and then the priestess declares the sacred circle open with the words:

And now let the feasting and libations begin!

Bewitched Movie Nights with Magickal Food

It's as simple as a charmed potluck and a good selection of magickal movies! Contributions to a charmed potluck include dishes that everyone brings that say something of themselves. So before eating, everyone introduces her dish and describes what it says of her and why she wants to offer it up to her sisters for their enjoyment.

One may bring a fresh green salad and offer it as representative of positive, fresh, new energies of love growing in each other's lives. Another may bring a sweet dessert, offering it as a way to sweeten everyone's love life.

Once everyone has introduced their dish and laid out the delicious spread, pop a magickal movie in the player and a bewitched evening is well underway!

Here are some of my personal classic movie favorites for a gathering like this—it's a broad selection but each features the essentials: magick, love, and seduction!

Bell, Book and Candle: The movie that inspired the TV series *Bewitched*.

The Mists of Avalon: The TV movie version starring honorary Witch Angelica Huston.

The Wicker Man: The original '70s English film. Although it was presented as being in the horror genre, it is actually an accurately researched representation of Pagan life in the part of the world that birthed it. Two of my favorite scenes are Britt Eckland's enchanting song and dance of seduction and the maidens jumping over the fire to encourage fertility.

Divine Secrets of the Ya-Ya Sisterhood: An inspiring movie of imagination and creation, women bonding as allies and inspiration to and for each other.

Love Actually: The sweetest and most gorgeous film about love manifesting beautifully, hilariously, tragically, and ultimately rewardingly in vastly different lives.

Practical Magic: Nicole and Sandra are great, but it is the eccentric aunts that Stockard and Diane play that really charm. The broomstick exorcism is one of my favorite scenes.

Chocolat: Features two of my all-time favorite things in great abundance: chocolate and Johnny Depp!

The Witches of Eastwick: Although it aligns magickal, powerful women with the Devil, how could Cher, Susan, and Michelle not enjoy the mischievous charms of Jack Nicholson?

After the movie, take the opportunity to chat about what was personally appealing about the film, and share with your sisters a recent positive experience in your own life that reflects this.

Witches' Tea Party

A Witches' tea party is a lovely way for the gals to get together for an afternoon of tea and treats—and bewitchery!

Step One

Send out an Evite or posted invite card to all your girlfriends. Here is an example:

Subject: Witches' Tea Party.

It's time to gather and share happy times
And bless our lives with good loving vibes
Dress to impress and arrive at the stroke of 2
And bring your dreams because they will come true

Dress:
Everyone must dress in magickally ladylike attire

Witch Tip

When I first hosted a Witches' Tea Party, I read everyone's tea leaves as a fun touch! If you don't have this skill, it is quite simple to learn. Get a book on tea-leaf reading and practice with lots of tea parties!

Food

A Witches' tea party is an elegant affair! Good English tea served in pots, little sandwiches, cakes and scones with jam and clotted cream are very appropriate.

Fine china and linen napkins are optional but will certainly enhance the experience.

The one obvious area where a Witches' tea party differs from the traditional English tea that inspires it is that some witchery will be performed. In addition to the tea and sweet treats, there will be small pink notecards and pens on the table.

Tea, then Witchery

Everyone enjoys their tea together, then the person hosting the party will signal that it is time to do some magick. She will invite each Witch to write her dream love scenario on one of the pink cards—anonymously. They can write as much or as little as they choose. It can be about how they want to improve their love life, a description of their ideal lover, or how they want to enhance an existing relationship. When everyone has finished writing, all the cards are placed in a cloth bag (a small pillowcase can also work for this).

The hostess then shakes the cards around a little and invites each person to reach in, take one out, and read it aloud.

The cards are written anonymously and read out in a sacred space of unified intent because you all want your dreams to come true, for yourself and each other.

As each card is read, it is placed in the center of the table. After the final dream is made known, the hostess places her right hand on top of the pile of cards. The next girl places her right hand on top of her hand, and so on, until everyone is connected by right hand to the pile of dreams. All then take a moment to close their eyes and focus on their desire to be truly happy and experience love abundantly.

The hostess then says these words, which the others repeat:

Our dreams are known

And are blessed with our intent

Our needs are met.

The cards are then placed back into the cloth bag and sealed with a pink ribbon to preserve the magick. The hostess "minds the magick" until the next Witches' tea party, which is when the cards shall be "released"—that is, burned in a pot or fireplace that is witnessed by everyone before recasting their spell. This makes way for new dream magick to be invoked by the bewitchers.

Enchanted Spoon Making

There is a great saying that if you want to change something in your life, you need to stir things up a bit—which is why I am going to introduce you to love spoons! The following event is a creative (Witch)craft workshop inspired by Welsh love spoons.

The ancient custom of giving love spoons dates to the sixteenth century. In Wales (one of the birthplaces of the Pagan rites and customs that we incorporate into our modern Witchcraft), these spoons were carved from a single piece of wood by a young man and presented to the girl he wished to marry. Decorative carvings were added to the spoon, the symbols having various meanings.

Many tourists return from Wales with a love spoon as a souvenir, and in modern times love spoons are considered great gifts for any occasion—weddings, anniversaries, birthdays, even housewarming presents—as they represent love and good wishes.

Witch Tip

When the cards are released, nothing negative happens. If, by chance, one of the Witches' dreams has not come true (which is highly unlikely), she will have the chance to re-request it as a part of the dream magick at the new tea party. If one of the sisters who attended the first tea party cannot attend the next, still nothing negative will happen when her card is released—she will have either had her dream come true by then or the act of releasing her card will allow a better-suited scenario to make itself known to her.

The love spoons in Wales are always individually hand-carved and not mass produced for the tourist trade. Each love spoon is a unique piece that is signed by the artist, who has conferred a little of their personal magic and intent into the act of making it.

I am not suggesting that the goddesses gathering for this event must be expert wood carvers. The love spoons that I am suggesting you make honor the original intent from when they first evolved in Wales, in that you are going to create an artistic effort with a spoon that will bless, empower, and "stir up" your love life in a positive way!

To Make Enchanted Love Spoons, You Will Need:

- Wooden spoons
- Crystals
- Felt-tip pens in various colors (silver blessed by moon energy and pink for love are good)
- Ribbons
- Charms
- Fast-drying paint
- Artist brush
- Non-toxic glue

Decorate your spoons with painted symbols, charms tied to ribbons from the handle, and crystals glued to the base. You can even paint or carve the names of your beloved or one you wish to love into your spoon to bless your union.

Have fun, be creative, and applaud each other's efforts as you create together—the more energy and enthusiasm you can raise as you create your love spoons, the more love will be stirred up in your lives!

Empowering the Love Spoons

A little empowering ritual for the love spoons is done together once everyone is satisfied with their efforts (and any glue and paint is dry so nothing will fall off or get smudged). A good way to ensure that nothing is knocked apart is to make the love spoons and leave them to dry for an hour or so. Use this as an excuse to open a bottle of wine (or three) and toast the bewitching goddesses that you are, after which you can do the empowering ritual before taking your love spoons home.

The Empowering Ritual: On the center of a table around which you can all stand, light four sticks of sweetly scented incense aligned with love energy—anything fruity and luscious will be perfect.

Stand or sit around the table with your love spoons in front of you. Hold hands and breathe in unison for a couple of minutes, allowing everyone's energy to ground and anchor each other in a sacred space of infinite love potential. Whoever has been chosen to lead the empowering ritual then says the following words:

> **With pure and honest intention**
>
> **We have forged our love spoons**
>
> **To stir up the potential**
>
> **For bliss and joy within our hearts**
>
> **And in the lives of those we charm.**

Then each person takes turns "stirring up" the incense smoke with their spoons as it spirals at the center of the table. The sacred smoke "smudges" the spoon—purifying it and empowering it for each person. When everyone has taken their turn, the person leading says:

> **The magic is spun**
>
> **Our will is done**
>
> **Love will come.**

Each bewitcher takes home her love spoon and places it next to her bed. Every morning upon arising she can take the love spoon and, facing the sun, "stir" the air in front of her heart three times in a sunwise direction (clockwise), saying:

Love is stirred

My needs are heard

It is done

Love shall come.

Anytime a bewitcher chooses to "stir up" some love energy in her life, she can pick up the spoon and give it a whirl, knowing that she is conjuring and creating her desires from the infinite potential for happiness in the universe around her.

A Love Healing Circle

This is simple and effective and can be incorporated into any gathering to help and heal each other's hearts.

Decorate the space with candles and fresh flowers, and ask that everyone wear something white. You will need:

- A big bowl of spring water with rose petals floating in it

- A cup of rose water added to the above bowl

- Some pink rose quartz crystals

- Soft white towels

Everyone washes their hands in the sacred water, drying them lightly on the towels. The first person to be healed sits

Witch Tip

Love spoon symbols evolved to vary widely from one locale to another in the country of their origin. The symbols were usually representative of the carver's life and interests. Remember, he would be making it to give to his sweetheart so that she would know of his life, his intentions, and his desire for her.

in the center, with the sisters gathered around comfortably in a circle. (Each person will take a turn sitting in the center of the healing circle.)

Everyone holds out their hands with palms facing toward the person, thus channeling positive healing energy. The person leading the ritual says the following words:

In love and light

Thou art blessed on this night.

Then each person takes a turn saying to the person being healed:

I, (Name), love you, (Name).

You don't need to worry about whether or not you are psychic or can channel healing energy to be able to do this circle effectively. The fact that everyone is there with a sincere desire to heal and empower will be magical enough. When everyone has offered their love, the person leading the ritual claps three times and says:

It is done

Love will come.

And the next person takes their turn in the center.

After everyone has been loved and healed, you can all eat and drink together and speak only of positive love experiences, happiness, and good times.

Every bewitcher can continue to recharge the magic of this ritual in their lives in the days to come by looking at themselves in the mirror, smiling, and saying, "Thou art loved."

Here are some love spoon symbols that you can carve, paint, or draw, and their meanings:

Heart: love

Key/keyhole: positive energy for your home and love living in it

Chain: the linking of lives in love—especially family and friends

Horseshoe: luck in all areas of love

Bell: wedding or happy anniversary

Flowers: love blossoming

Leaves: love rekindling

Vine or twisted stem: lives entwined in fidelity

How Spells Work

You may have noticed that I haven't filled this book with a million spells and rituals—yes, there are a few, but not *that* many! There is a reason for this.

Part of an eclectic coven's work is to create their tradition and research, collate, and most importantly create the rituals and spells that will form their practice. There are a gazillion books out there with spells and rituals—including all my previous books. Some of my favorites are recommended at the back of this book. I encourage you to compile a selection from these that inspires and excites you. Also please check out my enormous spell book at www.fionahorne.com. However, here I do want to write some personal musings on how, after nineteen years of practice, I think spells work.

This is something I have spent a lot of time thinking about. I am a very rational person by nature, and I have analyzed the processes that I think create the often utterly extraordinary results I have obtained—that is, spells cast to help others. Interestingly, spells cast for myself don't often have the same effect. I do a lot of rituals that make me feel good generally but I don't request specific results from them. Why this is so I will cover shortly.

People need to find the key that unlocks their individual belief that something extraordinary is possible. For some it is Witchcraft, for others not. Not everyone who goes to an Anthony Robbins seminar becomes a millionaire, but many do. In the same way, not every spell works, but many do. Science acknowledges that part of the world manifesting the way it does is because of the way we perceive it. We need to believe something extraordinary is possible in order to switch on the potential for what we want to manifest. That's why spells can work, because often the concept of them and the process of them stimulates something deep inside us. It triggers hope and awakens the child within, who once lived in a world full of enchantment, magick, and infinite possibilities.

Why Spells Cast By Me Work Best for Others

I do a lot more rituals for myself than spells, and there is a difference. A ritual is like building a home, and spells are the furniture you put in it. In my craft, I concentrate on building a strong home in which I can live, and people can visit and hopefully derive enjoyment and benefits from their time there.

Maybe this has to do with my lengthy years of practicing; perhaps it is appropriate now that I spend more time in service to others. But to do this the best I can I have to be spiritually strong, and that's where the rituals and observances (like my morning coven dedication) help.

Spellcasting is a powerful activity for all the reasons I mention above. But there is something more to it. There is power in the symbols, words, herbs, crystals, colors, numbers, and phases of the moon. That power manifests when we recognize it. If we look to it, it makes itself visible. For example, if I relate to an herb as a benign food source, then it will be just that. To work magick with it, though, I see it as a vibrating mass of energy particles, evolved of a planet that I too evolved of, sharing my life force, sharing the very same chemical molecules that I have making up my body, my reality, my consciousness. I can then align myself and interact with its power, harnessing it to assist me in manifesting my will.

Evolution of the species takes millions of years—with magick we can speed things up a bit, which is part of the magickal revolution. Look how talent develops in the human species when it is acknowledged and encouraged. Our athletes are fitter, stronger, and more capable than ever. And it's not just improved nutrition and training methods or illegal steroids—it is the mindset that we can be more extraordinary that is encouraged, that we can continually better the heights we reach.

As the modern Western world (re)awakens to the subtle energies of existence, psychic powers, kinetic powers, and all those "super" natural qualities that we have, so they will grow within us, becoming more present, more relevant, and more powerful.

As a species we must continue to evolve: death, destruction, pain, and suffering are all necessary in the cycles of life. But when these dark experiences are tempered with acceptance, honor, and respect, they cease to rule us and become trials of strength that we must face and embrace bravely, for they hold us together and give us a point of reference to encourage us to keep moving forward. Then we can know that love, goodness, and compassion manifesting as growth and enlightenment are the foundations upon which we build our lives and are the most powerful expressions of our existence in this extraordinary universe.

During the writing of this book I was working out at the gym one day when the TV screens above my head caught my eye. I generally never watch TV, but it was the sight of a news reporter with her lollipop pink suit and neatly coiffed brown helmet of hair giggling as she inexpertly handled an enormous Uzi machine gun that horrified me and stopped me in my tracks. Without a soundtrack, the vision, unjustified by words, was inexplicably macabre and sad. No doubt it was sensationalist reporting on the "terror threat." It was utterly surreal and highlighted to me that there really is no inherent power in a gun until a human decides to pick it up and fire it—even if it has been designed to kill and the vision of it inspires awe and fear. It reminds me of a scene that a good girlfriend of mine, Briane, a reporter for CNN in the Afghanistan war, shared with me.

Upon her arrival in Kabul, she entered the foyer of a hotel and spotted a large rifle casually propped up in the doorway. In its barrel was a single red rose.

Sharing this anecdote, I mean to demonstrate that it is our *perception* of the power of an object that confers it power—and this applies very much to the magickal tools of Witchcraft. It is your knowledge and comprehension of potential power and the way that you use it that determines the effect it can have. Your world will be as magickal as you let it be; as soon as you start doubting what you are doing and feeling that it is silly or rubbish, then it will be.

Another simple analogy I have often used to explain this is: imagine you are at a dinner party, sitting at a table with twelve other people, and everyone is speaking Italian. You don't speak Italian. You listen to the babble around you and watch the wild gestures and expressive movements of the people passionately talking, and it all seems a little ridiculous. You have barely any idea of what is going on. However, if you learn the language, suddenly a fascinating world appears, full of interesting stories, passion, excitement, and, most importantly, understanding.

It is the same for awakening your witchiness. Learn the language of magick and the world becomes a magickal place! That seemingly elusive, ethereal "otherworld" of real magick can be a lot closer than you think; it is inside you—in your desires, hopes, fears, and dreams. Open the door to that world inside you, and watch the world around you shift and change and shape itself to please you and be everything you dreamed it could be.

Tips from the Top

Here's a selection of general tips and ideas that may equip you to see obstacles as opportunities and trials as transformation.

Stick With It

The beauty of practicing the Craft, both as a solitary and as part of a coven, is that the experience becomes more textured, complex, and deep, yet easier as you go along. Persevere through the teething stages. What was once an effort to remember and organize shifts to become intuitive. You trust your gut, thus conjuring satisfying spiritual and magickal experiences effortlessly. It's as if you awaken an age-old sense of what it is to be human, the purest expression of the extraordinary life force of this universe.

Know that not even the smallest magickal act is wasted; they all contribute to the divine tapestry of life that we design for ourselves.

I Did It My Way

Don't feel you have to abide by someone else's way of doing things, as if they're standing over your shoulder, judging you. This is a hang-up left over (for most of us) from growing up in a patriarchal religion with the wrathful and vengeful "father" God sitting in the sky, judging us. You will never feel and experience real, tangible magick if you seek it solely outside yourself.

Just Chill

The more complicated and elaborate a ritual is doesn't necessarily mean it is more powerful. Be relaxed, confident, and deeply connected emotionally, spiritually, and physically with your intent. Then it will be more powerful and effective to simply light a red candle and make a wish for love than spend a whole day concocting an elaborate ritual, only to perform it feeling uncentered and distracted from worrying about getting it right.

Also, don't expect that the tingle of magick feeling has to go on for hours for it to be a sign that your spell has worked and that magick is indeed real. Magickal transformation occurs outside the physical construct of linear time, and you can indeed trust that you are experiencing infinite potential the moment a shiver goes up your spine or you feel different as the spell is cast or the ritual evoked.

I've Said It Before and I'll Say It Again

The only thing you need to believe in is yourself—trust your inner voice, trust your methods, trust your choices. You are a Witch, and that is enough.

Hey, This Is Fun!

As you and your coven spend more time together perfecting your craft, you may feel compelled to let your hair down and hang out, doing some fun and crazy stuff together. I mentioned in an earlier chapter that my coven and I don't socialize much together outside of our specific coven activities—but that doesn't mean you can't. There are lots of fun activities to do together that can enhance your bond in both this world and your covenworld.

Shopping

Shopping is always fun—but give the mall a miss and instead plan a day to go "magickal" shopping. Choose a cool witchy supply store to visit (there are names and locations on my website), and stock up on herbs, incenses, talismans, and crystals. Pick a witchy clothing store and buy new gear for your next full moon ritual; choose an identical ring or bangle for you all to wear as members of your coven; have lunch at a vegetarian café or restaurant, and wrap up the afternoon browsing the shelves in an esoteric bookstore.

Coven Reading Circles

Thanks to Harry Potter, it seems reading is no longer sliding into being a lost art. A reading circle is where you meet once a week to read an inspirational fictional book. I think a work of fantasy that has a magickal theme is particularly apt for a coven reading circle, as it will stimulate your collective imagination and so enhance your group visualizations and meditations. Choose a book (our first reading circle featured the classic *The Mists of Avalon* by Marion Zimmer Bradley), scatter furry rugs and beaded cushions on the floor, light incense and lots of tealight candles, and conjure a weekly night of enchantment and escape for you all to relish.

Attend Workshops Together

Learning about lots of different topics can enhance your craft. The Learning Annex (see appendix) offers terrific educational events nationwide where you spend a night with an instructor being introduced to a topic or skill. I conduct Witchcraft workshops for the Annex, and I attend their other workshops too. Making natural cosmetics, soaps, and candles are all skills I've found very helpful and enjoyable. More esoteric subjects have been palmistry, spoon-bending (like Uri Geller), and holotropic breathwork with the brilliant psychologist Stanislav Grof (which is basically how to achieve out-of-body states by breathwork).

Knitting Circle

Knitting hit Hollywood a few years ago as a cool hobby and its appeal hasn't let up. There is a powerful type of magick you may read about in various books on the Craft called cord magick. As cords are woven and knotted together, intent and will is sealed and enchanted in the cords.

Knitting can work the same way. You each knit squares, and as each one is completed you each hold it and chant an affirmation so that each square is empowered. A chant we like to use is:

Bound and blessed by sacred effort

This cord now weaves our dreams together

Sew the squares together and it is a coven blanket to meditate under together (just lie down and cover yourselves with it), or you could hang it in your temple space. Another cool idea would be to share it and each take it home one night to sleep under, receiving everyone's blessings and ensuring sweet and prophetic dreams.

Intuition Adventure

This is one of my faves! Get together and write a list of "directions," something like:

Go to the crossroads.

Walk north for five minutes.

Take four steps to the left and look for a power object.

Walk south for ten minutes.

Look to the sky for a sign.

The list is written purely spontaneously and intuitively—the idea is to see where you end up! It sounds bizarre, but try it and you'll see it's quite extraordinary. The list above is part of one that I created for a solitary intuition adventure. After meditating for about twenty minutes, I spontaneously wrote it. My power object ended up being a ring that was lying in the grass; it wasn't valuable, but it was pretty and made from a carved shell. The sign in the sky was a formation of clouds in the shape of the dragon tattoo on my arm.

When I got home, I wrote up the experience in my Book of Shadows. It always reminds me to focus on the journey, not the destination, as I travel through my life. Write a list of directions like this with your coven, go for a walk together, and see what magick you can uncover and experience together.

Adopt a Park

My biological mother, Erika, living in Australia, is an honorary Witch—she charms birds, literally. I have seen her hand-feed a wild kookaburra (a native Australian bird), and I've watched a magpie hop into her beauty salon in suburban Brisbane, not just by herself but with her young chicks in tow! To see Erika "speak" to the birds and to watch their heads cock and nod in return is one of the most uncanny and enjoyable sights! Erika is also a custodian of nature. She took the park which fronts her beauty salon under her wing (so to speak), as it was very neglected, with a threadbare carpet of grass and ailing plants. She personally picked up the rubbish and petitioned the council to fertilize the grass. The local paper wrote about her taking the park into her care, and that provided enough momentum for her request that a council re-plant be granted. In honor of her enthusiasm and care, the council planted butterfly-attracting bushes (butterflies are her favorite creature and the featured symbol in her beauty salon), and the park has now become a thriving ecosystem of not only plants, trees, birds, and butterflies, but also humans as they come to it to relax and enjoy the wonderful energy it emits under my mother's nurturing eye.

Why not do something similar in your coven? Choose a local park or a neglected plot of land—anywhere that you can work to heal and nourish the earth—and create an environment of beauty and harmony for all creatures to enjoy.

Pagan Holy Shrines

When I used to play in the Australian bush as a young girl I would make little magickal "hotspots" all over the place. I thought my little "natural art" creations would be nice for fairies to play in and be a pretty sight for any mortals who passed them by.

I would weave branches together into a canopy and place flat rocks underneath and scatter the area with pretty pebbles and flower petals. I would take a picture of a beautiful lady (I remember using pictures from a book I had of the remarkable '60s model Veruschka, who used to paint her body with images of nature like leaves and vines—"to disappear into it," she would say). I would then hang the image from a branch and tie feathers and flowers off the branches around it to create a "tree Goddess." Of course my little Pagan power spots were sometimes trampled or damaged, but more often than not they survived for ages. I made sure everything I used was biodegradable and recyclable and would just blend away into the nature they were formed from.

There is an incredible artist who creates works of art from nature using ice, water, flowers, wood, sand, stones, and leaves. Although he is not a Witch, his means and methodology are utterly Pagan. His name is Andy Goldsworthy, and there are books of his work and a profound film called *Rivers and Tides* (see appendix). If you feel inspired as a coven to create some natural magickal art, I highly recommend you look at his work for inspiration.

Camping Together

Or, as we say in Australia, "going bush"—that is, "getting away from it all." Especially if you live in a hectic urban environment, it is essential to recharge your witchy batteries. Go camping and set your tents up in a circle and together cast a sacred circle by studding the earth around your tents with crystals and shells to protect and empower your space. Light a fire in the center, burn incense at the doorway of each of your tents, and float flowers in water next to your sleeping bags, and you have invoked the four elements. Relax and recharge yourselves by communing with nature and making magick together.

Festivals and Gatherings

There are many festivals and gatherings all over the country, if you know where to find them. They are wonderful opportunities to connect with like-minded people. Some of my happiest witchy memories are from the gatherings I attended in Australia in my early "out" days. I wrote my first book, *Witch: A Magickal Journey*, around that time in my life; check it out, especially the part about "Wemoon," which was the first women-only gathering I attended and was particularly amazing.

For nationwide gatherings, again I recommend "The Witches' Voice" (www.witchvox.com) as a great way to find out what is happening. Also you can contact your local Pagan or New Age store to ask about events in your area and further afield that as a coven you may like to attend together.

Visiting Sacred Sites and Taking Magickal Holidays Together

North America is loaded with gorgeous destinations. As I recommend earlier in this book, why not visit Salem and pop into my friend Laurie Cabot's store for some witchy supplies, do trance meditation at the Joshua Tree, camp amongst the redwoods in Big Sur, go diving with the seals amongst the kelp forests of Southern California, and do a voodoo tour in New Orleans. (Well, these are some of the things I have done!) You are only limited by your imagination and your budget. If you travel as a coven together, make sure you keep a travel diary to record your adventures and magickal insights in—and take lots of photos!

Environmental Angels

Join a conservation group, whether that be for the environment, humanity, or for a particular cause you are passionate about—like perhaps breast cancer or stem cell research—and participate in activism and fundraising (visit my website, www.fionahorne.com, click on "about witchcraft" and then "gaia gateway" for lots more information and links). Give your acts a boost by casting a circle, raising white light power, and then drawing it back into yourselves before you head out on a cleanup or a fundraising drive so that you are beacons of healing light as you undertake your activities.

Room for Improvement

Sometimes, despite everyone's best intentions, there will be disagreements and problems in your coven, and it will be necessary to structure a kind of governing body.

This will also smooth out any other kinks and get a good working system going within the coven to support it in the physical realm.

The roles suggested in this chapter can be enacted individually or one person can perform two or more of the tasks, depending on the size of your coven. Having a governing body that can share leadership will facilitate a more harmonious and successful coven. As individual skills grow and the basic craftworking is perfected, everyone becomes more aware of their personal potential and wants to work harder. This can lead to ego struggles and personality clashes.

The Leader (or Leaders)

I always say that in the Craft everyone ultimately leads themselves, but part of leading yourself is making smart decisions about being guided by those who have more knowledge and experience that you can benefit from. In a traditional coven this would be the high priest and high priestess, but for an eclectic coven I think a term that conveys a less hierarchical structure is more appropriate. In my coven I am the leader, but I am referred to as just Fiona. For example, when I do my morning dedication I just say "I declare myself Witch of the Dark Light of Lilith coven," not "high priestess."

However, it is very clear I am the most experienced Witch and take the initiative in suggesting and creating most activities for the coven. As I say earlier, though, I do this with a view to ultimately sharing leadership.

The roles of the leader or leaders are essentially to:

- Teach the other coveners the ideology, skills, and practices of the Craft, particularly pertaining to the coven's way of doing things.

- Lead the rituals and spells of the meetings and suggest "home" work.

- Keep conversations between coveners moving harmoniously, making sure that everyone has a fair say and is heard and listened to.

- Oversee the spiritual health and growth of the coven as a whole.

- Advise individuals on positive development of themselves and on mental and emotional challenges that may be affecting their craft.

A Talking Stick

No, this stick isn't used for hitting someone over the head when you wish they'd shut up! It's a wonderful tool for when there is a potentially heated or emotional discussion taking place that ensures everyone has a fair say and feels they have been heard by the group. A talking stick doesn't have to be a stick per se, just an object that is clearly visible by all members of the coven. The way it is used is simple: as it is passed from person to person, it signifies that no-one else may speak except them.

In the tradition of high priestess and priest it may be a good idea to have two leaders, either female/male or same sex. In a traditional coven, the polarities of male and female are seen as of paramount importance. This is because Witchcraft was incepted as a fertility cult (as much as I dislike that word, it's appropriate here), and the sexual union of female/male was seen as the ultimate expression of the spiritual because it meant the tribe would continue to procreate and prosper. Hence the symbolic representation of the Great Rite (female/male sexual union) in most circles and the occasional actual lovemaking that takes place (see the chapter "You Sexy Witch!" for more on this).

However, in an eclectic coven it is unlikely that such overtly defined roles will be as appealing. Modern Witches know that the polarities of masculine and feminine exist in everyone regardless of gender, and Witchcraft has evolved to revere the life force as not only made manifest physically but mentally, emotionally, psychically, and spiritually.

One particularly good thing about an eclectic coven having two leaders is that you can share the workload!

The Coordinator

A coordinator is very necessary when a coven numbers more than three or four and the logistics of dates, times, locations, supplies, and appropriate clothing and food to be brought needs to be communicated accurately to everyone.

It is very good for when there is a large group and individual voices can be lost. A good rule of thumb is that everyone has to hold the talking stick during a discussion, thus everyone should express their thoughts on a situation so that no one hides their opinion and lets it simmer (which can brew potential problems later). It generally starts and ends with the leaders, so that they can initiate and sum up the discussion and necessary action pertaining to it.

The coordinator works very closely with the leader, using their initiative to assist the leader with innovative ideas for all of the above.

The coordinator:

- Assists the leader in planning coven rituals, events, and festivals.

- Keeps all contact details for each coven member.

- Has access to a computer and phone/fax for contacting people.

- Keeps a record of all successful and potentially successful locations for gatherings.

- Has the contact details for the local council and Pagan/Witchcraft groups that coordinate festivals and events that the coven may wish to take part in and/or contribute to.

- Works closely with the money person in regards to what coven supplies and stores are needed for ritual or are running low, if there is an established pantry of magickal goods.

The Money Person

This mathematically inclined person controls the funds of the coven and suggests and coordinates money-raising activities. Once a coven gets larger and more comfortably established, it may make sense to all contribute an amount of money each week to go toward various things, like supplies and food for gatherings or perhaps transport (like a rental car) for magickal excursions, and fees for locations (like a rented hall). If you are really cashed up, this could mean airfares and accommodation costs for magickal excursions and holidays.

The money person:

- Collects and perhaps banks contributions from coven members.

- Keeps track of spending and distributes funds as necessary for supplies and travel.

- Suggests innovative ways for making money—perhaps raising funds by selling things at festivals and markets.

- Keeps the inventory of a coven supply pantry of herbs, incenses, candles, and other items used in ritual.

The Book Worm

Keeping the coven's Book of Shadows updated can be a big job, and having an individual particularly devoted to this can be a bonus, especially if they have artistic skills! As instructed by the leader, this person maintains the coven's Book of Shadows by:

- Writing up and/or pasting in ritual reports, spells, coven member names and other details, and whatever else is deemed appropriate.

- If there is a coven book/DVD/video/CD library, the book worm can also run the lending system.

The Activist

This proactive and highly motivated person keeps on top of the coven's environmental and service activities, suggesting causes to champion and activities to perform.

The activist:

- Maintains the coven's membership to environmental causes like Greenpeace, Planet Ark, Project Aware, and humanitarian causes like sponsoring developing-world children.

- With the coordinator, the activist arranges for the coven to perform appropriate activities of activism and service.

Internet Covencrafting

You need to be flexible when you are part of a coven. In the old days when there were no planes, trains, or automobiles, it was a safe bet that everyone physically stayed pretty close to one another. Nowadays it is another story, but we have the Internet to help us stay close, not to mention SMS and video phone messages! The Internet transmits human thought as light and 0s and 1s—these are proven potent magickal forces!

The Webmistress/Master

It can be terrific for your coven to have its own website for you all to enjoy, and if you are lucky enough to have a web designer in your group, this can be a reality. It can contain an online Book of Shadows for everyone's reference and a member's forum for you to chat online when you are physically apart. Witches and Pagans are generally very Internet savvy, and our craft has evolved to embrace technology as a potent means of communication, both physically and metaphysically. When gathering together physically becomes difficult, the Internet keeps everyone connected and committed to maintaining the covenworld.

Keep It Fresh

Maintaining some of your solitary methods and practices in addition to those you share with your coven is important. The benefits of this are far reaching. If everyone does everything exactly the same, a coven can become stagnant. Individual members bringing their personal revelations and suggestions are essential to maintaining a vital and ever-evolving coven. As I've mentioned before, at home I have my personal altar and my coven shrine. This keeps me connected to my individual magickal self as well as the collective that I am a part of in my coven. I do work with the coven, but I also do spells and rituals that I do not involve the coven with. I have more to offer my coven the more I grow and expand as a Witch individually.

I feel this is a very important point to make. Never forget that we Witches are individuals—we do not have to be the same as each other nor share exactly the same opinions or look the same; in fact, it is essential that we don't. So don't be defensive when others within your coven disagree. It's a healthy sign of people thinking for themselves, again essential for Witches. However, if their behavior is more akin to that of a wanker than a Witch, read on . . .

How Do You Know When Someone Has to Go?

Fortunately, this hasn't happened to me—we are mature women who are smart and confident enough to work through any issues calmly and constructively. Confidence is usually a factor when someone is acting like an idiot. Having to over-assert your presence or your opinion is usually a cry for attention, because deep down the individual feels that they are not really that great and worthy of attention.

However, I have had to exercise some "cut the crap" action on my website's forum where I am an administrator. When it was first set up, we had a visitor who seemed intent on creating havoc. They wrote abusive and ignorant things about me, and insulted other forum members by loudly proclaiming themselves as a "real" Witch and an authority on "their" religion, dismissing other people's contributions and witchy identities.

I have conducted several successful online rituals: fiber-optic cable and the power of words seem to convey intent and will very successfully to create change. The rituals involved the members being online at the same time, typing their intent, punctuated with certain colored symbols and posting them on a forum especially established for the purpose.

Psychic skills are not bound by time and space in the three-dimensional world, so being in the same physical space is not always necessary for certain covencrafting. See the "Making Magick Together" chapter for more information on this.

A lot of concerned messages were being posted by the established forum members, concerned that the nasty things being said about me would upset me. I wasn't upset because I knew this person was just immature, insecure, and attention-seeking, and I posted a message relaying this. I was concerned that the forum members were upset, so I asked them if they would like me to block/erase the inflammatory posts.

A lot of people wrote that everyone has the right to their opinions, but this had gone beyond that. So the other administrators and I erased all the ignorant, vulgar comments. The particular individual became very contrite and settled down, then actually started to constructively contribute—and, of course, we welcomed them.

Here is a checklist: if there is a "yes" answer to three situations, I would recommend the person is in need of a severe warning of excommunication. If there is a "yes" to four situations, I would recommend that they leave.

- Deliberately starts arguments that are not constructive.

- Is physically invasive of other people's space.

- Makes unwanted sexual advances.

- Insults individuals personally and denigrates their efforts.

- Does not respond to other coveners' (especially the leader's) concerns about their behavior.

- Is lazy and repeatedly does not turn up at meetings or take part in coven activities (a couple of times with good reason is okay; after that, it is a problem).

I may sound a little idealistic, but I am confident that if the particular qualities of a Witch—these being personal empowerment, tolerance and respect, patience and compassion—are exercised, then kinks can always be ironed out. From a difficult situation can come new insights, growth, and strength . . . that's the theory anyway!

When you're deciding whether someone has to go, try not to take anything they are doing personally—*they* are the injured one. Witches are healers and sometimes to heal someone you have to make them aware of their problem, but this may mean excommunication.

Once you make a decision on this, stick to it. Have a set period of, say, six weeks that they are utterly excommunicated for; by this I mean if they start asking that they rejoin a week after they are kicked out, say no. A six-week minimum will test their sincerity and ensure they are not just wheedling their way back to entertain themselves in a sick way.

If they are sincere in their desire to contribute constructively to the coven and have learned from their mistake after six weeks, then re-initiate them with a joyful ceremony that celebrates their positive growth as an individual. The coven will only benefit from it.

You Sexy Witch!

Witchcraft is a fertility religion and a spiritual path. Sex is sacred, magick is sensual, and if you have any hang-ups about sex and sensuality, you may have trouble being an adept Witch.

Whether as Witches we incorporate our sexual practices into our rituals (be it solitary, with a partner, or even in a coven situation) or whether we simply insist on treating sexuality as one of life's great treasures rather than something debased or somehow impure, the magick of our physical selves is a matter of reverence and respect. This often causes those who have a vested interest in either repressing or exploiting sexuality to claim that Witches and Pagans have an attitude toward matters of the flesh that would make Austin Powers look like a celibate monk!

In fact, although Witches see a positive virtue in the blending of physical and spiritual happiness, the way this is expressed in individual lives varies widely. You'll find no shortage of monogamous, polygamous, gay, straight, bisexual, and even celibate Witches. Where the Craft differs from many other spiritual paths is in its refusal to claim that any one of these expressions is the One True Right and Only Way to live our lives.

Is it true to say that Witches are less prone to sexual jealousy and possessiveness than most people? Well, it's probably true to say that we try a lot harder to keep that sort of negativity at bay and maximize our happiness and that of the people we love. Like everyone else with an intact conscience, though, we do try to find a balance between our own needs and our lovers'. The Witch's Pyramid (To Know, To Dare, To Will, To Be Silent), after all, stresses that we should enact our will in such a way that we don't cause harm.

Conventional sexual attitudes can be hard to shift, however. Many of us have them drummed into us at very tender ages and despite our quests for freedom can find some of this indoctrination hard to shake. How, for example, would you feel if you had a partner and they took part in a magickal sex ritual to honor Beltane by enacting the Great Rite with someone other than yourself? To me and to many other Witches and Pagans (but—and I stress this—not all), there is a big difference between sex in ritual and sex with someone you love and who is your life partner.

Having said that, I will add that in reality, rituals involving actual sex are much rarer creatures than certain ill-informed and sensationalistic journalists would try to convince the world, and there are absolutely no obligations for Witches who are in covens or in any other situations to have ritual sex with each other. It is utterly a matter of choice, and whether or not your magick involves any form of sexual expression has no bearing on your power as a Witch. If you enjoy raising power through your sexuality, your magick will benefit from it, but if it's simply not in your nature to do this, forcing yourself can only have a negative effect on your workings. Powerful sex magick occurs when the participants are mature, experienced, and grounded in matters of life, love, and love-making. This rules out teenagers, the emotionally fragile, and disturbed power-trippers and egocentrics. Inside the circle and outside, never allow anyone to persuade you to do anything sexually that you really do not want to do. By allowing this, you undermine your self-respect and your magick.

The Great Rite

Some of the ancient tribal practices that are part of our witchy origins involved fertility festivals, where it was seen as essential to mate with others who were either not necessarily well known to you or were masked to conceal their identities. The sexual rites of Beltane—basically sex in the fields to ensure the fertility of the next season's crops—were a very holy event. Genetics weren't really understood at the time, but our ancestors had enough insight to realize that the survival of our species depended on the diversity of the tribe.

Although these archaic rituals aren't an integral part of modern Witchcraft, they still resonate within the practices and attitudes of modern Witches. In general practice, the uniting of a Wiccan circle's high priestess and high priest's bodies doesn't physically take place in the ritual, but is represented by the symbolic union of female and male through the chalice (female) and the athame (male)—in ritual we say "that which is female and that which is male; conjoined, you are the forces that shape all creation"—are united to represent the act of sex. It's as simple as that. Simple in its magnificence, the passion of love on all levels—matter through to spirit in this world and all the worlds above, below, and in between—is at the heart of what we do and who we are.

However, most Witches know a thing or two about how to raise magickal power and its similarity and interrelationship with raising sexual power. As a mature Witch, however, I find all Witchcraft ritual profoundly sensual and rooted in the ecstatic experience that is orgasm. When I raise energy in a cone of power, I find that it reflects the pattern of energy-conjuring and release of orgasm. Energy builds up to an ecstatic peak that explodes—floating over, in, throughout, and around all things—and then there is the gentle settling of the spark that started it all until it is anchored to the earthly realm again. All this is a mirror of the buildup/release/winding down expression of energy that is orgasm.

The good news is that if you're drowning in hormones, certain witchy rituals will have you on cloud nine! Rather than saying a prayer at night, have an orgasm (alone or with your partner) and offer the energy to the universe, where it can be put to even more good use.

In any solitary magickal working, I find virtually nothing beats using the energy of orgasm to fuel a spell to fruition or to seal the intent of a ritual. Also, when the orgasmic energy is forged in the act of lovemaking between two committed, loving partners, it is utterly mind-blowing and a sure-fire recipe for success.

In both cases, though, remember to treat the raising of sexual pleasure and power reverently. That doesn't mean you can't go absolutely wild with passion, but it does mean that you shouldn't make the working a pretext for having sex. Also, as you progress along the path of your awakening sacred sexuality, don't push yourself too hard when trying to dispel areas of sexual repression. For example, many of us are taught to be very shy about nakedness, so if working skyclad (naked) with friends seems daunting, get used to it by being naked at home alone or with your partner to help normalize it. Perhaps progress to other non-sexually threatening situations like skinny-dipping at a nude beach or being nude at a Pagan festival before trying the strange intimacy of a coven circle. Discuss any nervousness with the group (for instance, some guys, especially younger ones, might be embarrassed at the thought of inadvertently conjuring up an erection mid-ritual, and would need reassurance that it's perfectly fine if he does).

A lot of people have an ingrained sense of negativity about masturbation too, so when considering using it in ritual, get a lot of practice in first! Learn to enjoy it and erode away any attitudes of guilt or embarrassment before attempting it to empower a spell. Similarly, if you're trying sexual magick with a partner, first have lots of non-ritual sex! Nervousness and awkwardness aren't going to help your magick, so get very comfortable with each other's bodies before hitting the circle. Take turns pampering each other, watching each other masturbating (a powerful way to learn what your partner most enjoys), and most especially communicating.

Of course, the beauty of studying sexual magick is the fact that the homework is a whole lot more pleasant than most. So study hard and enjoy!

Questions from the Forum

There is a forum on my website where I invited people to post any questions they had about coven finding, coven forming, coven maintenance . . . coven anything, really!

I was flooded with all kinds of questions, spanning topics like "How do I find a coven to join?" . . . "How do you deal with problem people in a coven?" . . . "How do I get my parents to understand what I do?" . . . "How do I dismantle a coven?"

These are just some of the many questions (and answers)!

Uh-Oh, We've Hit a Rough Patch

What do you do when people in the coven start to argue about everything, from casting a circle to invoking deity? I have seen this happen and most covens just seem to break up. It would be good if someone could explain how to mediate for the coven members or something.

What you describe is a common problem. As much as everyone tries to promote the witchy principles of tolerance, compassion, and respect, sometimes you can't help but rub each other the wrong way. I discuss how to deal with the problems you mention in detail in the chapter called "Room for Improvement," but I can add here that sometimes it's important to take a moment out from everything and meet on neutral ground. Maybe you could all agree to go to a beach and just sit and have a talk about why you started the coven in the first place. What were your hopes? Try to connect back to that enthusiasm you had when you all decided to get together and try something. Don't talk about what has been going wrong or the problems that seem to have evolved; just focus on that early feeling. When you are all resonating strongly with that, suggest that you treat all obstacles as opportunities for change. Just because you are having problems now doesn't mean you always will. Look at your problems as good things to have because they are the doorway to you all becoming more powerful Witches. Sort these out and share the responsibilities of doing so, and you will be opening up to a greater sense of individual and collective self.

> I have never been a member of a real coven, with high priest and high priestess, but I have been in a few groups (like teen covens) and in the end we would always split up. It was always for the same reason. In time we would start to argue, but that wasn't the problem. The real reason was that there were always one or two power-hungry individuals who wanted to be in charge and to play the role of high priest or priestess, although everybody knew that nobody wanted the group to have the hierarchical structure like big covens.
>
> Now I'm in a group with a few friends of mine and my question is: how can we know in the future when somebody else comes to our group that that person is not self-centered and power-hungry? Is there any divination method or spell to know what that person's real intentions are?

I would say straight up that if you are having any really strong doubts at all from the start, then you should listen to your intuition and perhaps decide not to link up with this person in the first place. If you follow some of the suggestions in the "Bring It On" chapter about finding other members (checking astrological sign compatibility, for example), that can be a good start. You could get a pendulum kit and see if it swings toward or away from their name once you have posed the question to it. I think, though, that the best insight I can offer here is that "the world answers according to the questions you ask of it." If you expect people to "change" and be power-mad or difficult, then you are creating a ripe environment for them to do so. Try to be impartial and give everyone a fair go. You will find that everything will run more smoothly and positively.

How Can I Find a Coven?

How do you find a coven to join? I live in the city and don't hear much about them, and I'd really like to join one so I can learn a lot more about the Craft. I would be very glad if you were to put this in your book.

Once you start searching, you should not have too much trouble finding any number of established covens. I strongly recommend that you start by contacting the organizations I have listed at the back of this book. Another good idea is to visit your favorite esoteric bookshop and leave a notice there saying that you are looking for like-minded people to work with. Magazines like *newWitch* (available at good newsstands and bookstores) are also terrific contact points, and check out the forums on different websites. Mine has an active forum and there are links to lots of other witchy websites, including to the ones suggested at the back of this book.

Finding a coven that you fit into and enjoy may prove to be a little more challenging than making the initial contact. Keep an open mind and don't expect everything to be perfect straightaway. One of the most rewarding possibilities of being a coven member is that upon working through and solving problems you gain a greater appreciation and respect for everyone, and this leads to a greater appreciation and respect for yourself.

What is the safest and easiest way to join a coven?

Safety is a good point to make—I was disturbed once when there was an email posted on my website's Forum from a person who said he was the leader of a coven and insisted that sex rituals were a necessary part of initiation. I can't stress strongly enough that anything to do with sex and nudity is *not* a prerequisite of Witchcraft—and this goes five hundredfold for teenagers. As Witches, our bodies and our sexualities are sacred and divine and not to be used or exploited by anyone. Never, ever do anything that makes you feel uncomfortable. We erased this person's posting from the forum immediately and happily they didn't return. But you must always exercise caution; basically, the same rules apply to Witchcraft as for everyday life. Never agree to meet someone that you have met on the 'net alone. I have to say that out of all the people saying they are Witches, there is unfortunately a tiny percentage who are twisted and out to exploit and hurt people. However, from what I've seen, there are more in other mainstream religions, who form radical factions, pervert the teachings of the faith, and seek to willfully harm and mislead others.

I will again recommend contacting the organizations I have listed at the back of this book as a good place to start meeting people safely.

To be seen as a true witch do you have to belong to a coven?

No, you don't have to be a member of a coven to be considered a "true" Witch. You are a true Witch if you connect with the principles of Witchcraft as a way of physical, emotional, mental, and spiritual life. I discuss this in the chapter "What a Witch Is."

Teen Traumas

I have always had a close connection with the earth. My back yard is literally part of a protected woodland, so they aren't allowed to build houses there. I used to go playing out there when I was little. Then I read your books, which brought out the "witchiness" in me. The problem is, my friend Sara decided a week before I read your books that she wanted to become Wiccan. I'm scared that if I tell her, she'll think I'm copying her or following some fad. Also, my other friend Kate says she's Wiccan, but she just uses it to make herself distant to her family. Basically she does it to tick her parents off. My father has been getting on my nerves because I don't want him to find out that I'm Wiccan. My mother knows and totally accepts it, but my parents are divorced, and I'm staying with my father for two weeks. I hate not being able to do anything, because I don't have my altar (it's at my mother's house) and I can't make a subtle altar because even that he'd notice.

I'm wondering if there might be any teen covens that I'd be able to join. I don't know if I could find enough that live around me, but it would be nice.

You sound like me when I was growing up, playing in the bush and uncovering my inner witchiness! You also sound very young and I have to say to you that a lot of the things you imagine as problems are just that—imaginary. Be proud to tell your girlfriend that you too are Wiccan. An important part about being a Witch is not to have to prove anything to anyone except yourself. Be confident and happy to share your interests with her, and perhaps even use this book as a guide to forming a teen coven together!

Regarding your other friend, she is on her own journey and it is not your business to judge or change her. She will learn what she needs to. You should just focus on being the best you can be for now and know that you're fortunate that your mother understands and supports your choices as a Witch. However, as a teenager it's important that you respect your father, so don't parade your craft around in front of him to antagonize him, and don't resent his lack of acceptance. Remember you can carry your altar within your heart.

Experience the element of fire in the setting sun; the element of water in the ocean, a river, or the rain; the element of air in the breeze; and the element of earth under your feet by walking barefoot on the grass. The Goddess and God are within you. You have everything you need as a Witch right there.

My friends and I started a coven after reading your books. When I told my mom, she told me "No, it's too dangerous." When I asked her what she meant, she said, "Covens are dangerous, people do dangerous things and I don't want you to be a part of it. And I don't want you doing drugs." I tried explaining to her that a coven isn't a group of druggies or crazy people, and we don't worship Satan, but my mom is one of those people who won't listen. How can I get her to realize I'm serious and it's perfectly safe (and we don't kill people, she said that to me later)?

My book *Witchin'* has a section that addresses parents' concerns like the ones you mention. And in this book, the chapter "What a Witch Is" clears up any misconceptions. Suggest to your mother that she read about what real modern Witchcraft is and then you could perhaps have an informed discussion about it. Tell her you love her and understand that years of negative stereotyping has led her to think these things, but you really can promise her that Witches work for the good of all, with harm to none.

It's Over, Red Rover

My question is, how do you dismantle a coven? Most books that I have read on the Craft talk about forming covens and suggest formal rituals you can do, but none of them seem to suggest how to end a coven . . . any ideas?

You bring up a very good point. How are covens dismantled? Often there are strong bonds both psychically and physically. It should be known, though, that psychic bonds will gradually disperse if they are not continually reenforced. If the split is amicable, suggest that someone keep the Book of Shadows in safekeeping. Have a final gathering together that is more of an honoring ceremony, a bit like a wake in a sense in that you share food and drink and speak of the good times you shared and the lessons you learned together. Do not cast a circle or do any magick at this gathering. Farewell each other respectfully and walk away without looking back.

If the split is really unpleasant, bury the Book of Shadows to earth the negativity and do not have any contact with the other coveners whatsoever. If you find you are traumatized at all, burn a white candle at the doorway of the room you sleep in and sprinkle salt under the bed for twenty-one days to release the negativity and free you to move on.

Solitary Strength

I'm not sure what I would do if I was to be approached by a coven . . . I have been a solitary practitioner for almost two years now, mainly making a "book Witch" name for myself. Would a coven change the way my magick is enforced?

You're under no obligation to join a coven if they approach you—it's entirely up to you. A coven would change the way you practice, but you can keep up your solitary practices too, if you like (and have the time). Joining a coven should enhance your craft. If you have any doubts, don't do it. You are still a real Witch whether you're a book Witch or the high priestess of the Umpteenth Moon!

A couple of years ago, I went to a summer solstice gathering and had one of the most amazing magickal experiences of my life. It was beautiful, and it was my first time working with a group. What made it so special was that it was so informal. My biggest problem with Christianity is the utter rigidity of worship, and that's why I love being a solitary practitioner so much—there's no set form. I understand that a lot of covens insist on doing everything "by the book," so to speak. Is this true?

It's true some traditional covens are very pedantic about doing things "by the book." Covens whose practices are derivative of Gardnerian and Alexandrian traditions are an example. However, as I have made clear in this book, an eclectic coven is one that is more fluid and versatile and relies on the input of the individual members and how they express themselves as integral to its practices. Use this book as a guide to forming an eclectic coven, and you can continue to enjoy the spontaneity and fluidity of solitary practice with the bonus of added input from other like-minded souls.

Sorry if this is a silly question, but it just occurred to me that I may find it difficult getting into a coven because while I am a Witch I do not class myself as Wiccan. I'm following a different and I guess somewhat personal path. Would that make it difficult to join in with group work?

My own personal practices are quite eclectic and not strictly Wiccan, but my coven practices as Wiccan and I enjoy the variation. If you are interested in group work, perhaps suggest to some friends that you form a "working group" first rather than a coven, and dip your toe in the water, so to speak, to give working with others a try before committing to a formal coven.

My only question about covens is whether the members of a coven would look down on those who practice solitary.

If they do, they're wankers, not Witches. Just ignore them!

I Couldn't Say It Better Myself!

I am glad that the point of searching for covens has been brought up, because it is often a difficult task. However, you should definitely not worry that you are doing it "wrong" because there is no such thing. Many Witches in their early stages try to find "the only" way of doing things, but there is just not one way. As each of us are different and have different situations surrounding us, magick is extremely flexible. I have found that it is not the way you do things but the intentions behind them that counts, and if you believe in what you are doing and it works for you, then don't worry about the technicalities. One of the most important lessons to learn is to trust your instincts, so if it feels right, then do it!

Homework

Being a Witch is a 24/7 gig, and aligning with each other by sharing practical lifestyle approaches will greatly help you in developing your craft. I think these approaches should include:

- Experiencing responsible and healthy living by taking care of yourself: eating organic foods, recycling, using alternative health remedies, thinking healthy thoughts, and practicing healthy actions.

- Taking part in community service and environmental and social activism.

Healthy Living

I am a big advocate of organic food and vegetarianism, though over the years I have gone from being vegan to eating meat to vegetarianism. I think flexible eating and living habits are the most successful and allow you to be magickal as well as integrated in the everyday world.

By no means do you have to be vegetarian to be a Witch. I know lots of Witches who love big, hearty, meaty meals! But most Witches I know have very particular attitudes to the meat that they eat. They will only eat organic and sustainably farmed animal products, for example, free-range chicken and eggs; or they will only eat fish they have caught themselves. They do not eat at McDonald's because their methods of mass production go against witchy ethics. But even as a vegetarian, I think it is natural for humans to want to eat meat. If I am scuba diving and a shark wants to take a bite out of me because it is hungry, then so be it—in its world, I am food. I think it is fair for humans to consume other species as part of the natural order. But when we create genetically modified food, when we over-fish oceans and over-farm land and over-breed animals only to slaughter them, then we are not respecting the cycles of life on this planet.

As Witches, I think we should try to tread as gently as possible on the land, perhaps by growing our own foods and shopping at smaller, decentralized cooperative markets. We should also buy organic food at supermarket chains and increase the demand for it. We shouldn't eat fast food that is mass-produced with enormous waste and little nutritional value.

Respect the sacrifice an animal or plant makes by eating it reverentially and with consideration of its sacred life force that is being absorbed into yours. Your magick will improve, as will your physical appearance, when you eat well and with reverence.

Last year I gave my whole eating plan an overhaul. I had drifted back into eating fish and even meat sometimes. I was rundown and often eating sweets for energy. I was not paying attention to the quality of the food I was putting into my body, and I realized it was time for another overhaul (there have been a few in my time on this planet!). Following are some tips from me on healthy eating that you may like to incorporate into a coven makeover plan. If you all work to improve your eating, you can support and encourage each other as you adapt to the changes.

At home you have control over what you eat, so make your kitchen a temple of wholesome foods created and combined with love (one of the most nutritional substances around!). When I started my revised eating plan, my taste buds started to crave the overly sweet and salty foods they were accustomed to. But after a couple of weeks, extremely healthy eating became second nature and now, except for the occasional premenstrual attack of soy ice cream and dairy-free vegan organic chocolate, I find it easy to only eat healthily and selfishly. I say "selfishly" because when I eat well, it makes me feel fantastic—and I'm worth it. I don't care what people say to me when I'm in a restaurant and I won't eat the oily, meaty egg rolls with them.

So do some research and find organic, cooperative supermarkets and food stores near you. Patronize restaurants that serve organic food or vegetarian food. Have your general coven get-togethers at these places. Exercise the power of your consumer dollar and buy organic, locally produced products as much as possible. Yes, it's a little more expensive, but the more you buy, the more demand you create and, eventually, the prices will be lower.

Getting In Physical and Spiritual Shape

The following tips are *not* a diet—they are more to encourage you to think about what you put into your personal temple: your body. As a Witch, you have the power to be whatever you will, so get really excited about the fact that you have the power to re-create your health and physical state by eating well, and make decisions on what you eat based on this positive, empowered feeling.

As I write this, I am about to turn forty years old, and I honestly look and feel the best I ever have in my life. I am fitter, stronger, healthier, and (dare I say!) sexier than ever before. I attribute it to my outlook on life as a Witch—the power of my will combined with a lifestyle that is in harmony with the earth and the energies of magick. As I've already mentioned, when I am at home I am vegetarian and I only use organic everything. Even my tampons are organic cotton. (Okay, I'll stop—too much information! But I will say I don't flush them down the toilet, and at bedtime I use rewashable pads.) My home is my sanctuary, devoted to making me feel the very best I can in every way—physically, mentally, emotionally, and spiritually—and it supports me so that I tread lightly on this beautiful earth.

Some Really Handy Tips

Read labels: Help yourself make healthier food choices by studying food labels and avoiding those products that are high in fat, sugar, or salt. Also check that items are free of genetic modification and made from organic produce.

Eat more fresh foods: Processed foods are more likely to be high in fatty and sugary ingredients, while fresh, whole foods are low in these and high in beneficial vitamins, minerals, and other nutrients.

Note: The following recommendations about diet and food are based on my own eating plans. For more information about nutrition, veganism, and vegetarianism, consult a reputable handbook or cookbook that describes how to eat foods in combination so that you are receiving optimum vitamins, minerals, and nutrients for your busy witchy lifestyle!

Try to Eat More:

Fresh fruit: It's all good. Try to eat the equivalent of three fist-sized amounts a day.

Vegetables: Make sure you eat a wide variety, including sprouts and dark lettuce leaves. Again, it's all good, including avocado. Try to eat most of your veggies raw or steamed, not boiled or fried.

Fish: I don't eat fish anymore, as our oceans are overfished and fish populations decimated. I recommend that you no longer eat fish until an environmentally aware method of fish farming is introduced into the human food supply system.

Soy products: Like tofu, tempeh, seitan. Try to eat the equivalent of two fist-sized amounts a day if you're not eating meat. Watch out for some of the processed soy foods, though, like vegetarian hotdogs, as they can have lots of salt in them. Again, read the labels.

Nut products: Like nuts themselves (but no peanuts—they are a legume, not a nut, anyway), and no roasted, salted nuts. Also other products like almond butter and almond cheese.

Legumes: Like lentils, kidney beans, black beans, and soy beans—they're all good.

Seeds: Sunflower seeds, pepitas, and sesame seeds (including tahini) are excellent. Sprinkle them on your salad and veggies.

Whole-grain bread: Have a big salad sandwich with baked tofu and almond cheese for lunch.

Whole-grain pasta: Great for energy and fiber.

Cereals: Like oats, barley, quinoa, and brown rice.

Oils: Olive oil is brilliant as long as it's organic and virgin (and expensive!); coconut is okay for doing a light stir-fry (olive usually burns when it is overheated).

Garlic: A special mention. Eat lots of it, it's good for you! (You can eat parsley after it so you don't stink!)

Try to Eat Less:

Salt: Try not to add it or put it on anything. It's already added to so many foods (healthy ones included) that you'll get enough without adding anymore.

Dairy: You can substitute cheese, ice cream, yogurt, and butter/margarine with low-fat soy, almond, and rice products.

Meat, chicken, and eggs: If you're getting enough protein from soy and nut products (and perhaps fish), you won't need to eat much of these. However, if you choose to, make sure it's free-range and organically farmed.

Processed anything: For example, crackers, cakes, etc. If you need something sweet, call a good friend and have a nice chat or pick up a pet and give it a cuddle.

Sugar: Use honey, maple syrup, or rice bran syrup instead.

A few words on:

Alcohol: Not much, and only the good stuff.

Drugs: Yuk and boring! Magick is much more interesting and fun.

Cigarettes: Putrid, foul, and plain stupid.

Easy Coven Cooking

If you are in a coven, simple foods work best for the post-circle feast. One of my faves is a massive "Everything but the Kitchen Sink" salad. I get a bag of pre-washed organic mixed salad leaves and throw it into a large bowl. Then I toss in a handful of organic red and yellow cherry tomatoes and chop up some organic baby carrots. I grab a slab of teriyaki-baked organic tofu, chop it into cubes, and throw that in, plus a handful of sprouted lentils, some chopped almond cheese, and pine nuts, pepitas, or pecans. I toss a couple of dessertspoons of low-fat organic salad dressing and serve it with some pita bread and hummus. It's a great feed: delicious, filling, utterly good for everyone and incredibly quick.

It has to be said that I am a little spoiled living in America because we really do have the most amazing supermarkets here. Two in particular are Whole Foods and Erewhon—they are both jam-packed with organic and vegetarian/vegan food.

I would definitely encourage you to eat home-prepared foods after circle gatherings and at sabbat celebrations; don't just buy takeout food from the local Chinese restaurant and bring that along. One of the most important reasons not to eat takeout too much is that there is no love in it. When you make food for yourself or someone who cares about you makes food for you, it has love in it that is very nurturing. Your body will sense it, and your heart and health will blossom in response. Cooking is like spellcasting—there is alchemy involved, blending different things together and concocting new tastes, sights, and smells—so nurture this skill within your coven life.

The Superfit Coven

I've mentioned before that I generally don't socialize with my coven members, but that's just me. A lot of covens, particularly teen covens, will enjoy bonding together, both inside their sacred circle and outside. You could plan a coven fitness activity once a week or fortnight; perhaps take a yoga class together or hike in a really beautiful location. When you get to the top of the hill, you can all meditate together, or, if you have enough energy, raise power and burn a few more calories! My coven, as I write this, is planning to do a trek through the Joshua Tree National Park in the next month—that should be amazing! We'll be working up a sweat and meditating on the stark spiritual beauty of the place at the same time.

Witchy Health

If you are feeling really sick, it's always a good idea to visit the doctor. I must admit, I rarely go to a doctor—if I'm coming down with a cold, I take echinacea and vitamin C. I tend to rattle a bit with all the vitamins I take; I take seven pills and capsules twice a day! These are: a multi-vitamin, evening primrose oil, flaxseed oil, vitamin C, glucosamine (for my knee joints, they're trashed from dancing in my band for years), coenzyme Q-10 (anti-aging!), and St. John's Wort. The stress of living in America and the difficulty involved in working in the entertainment industry sometimes makes me depressed, so I take St. John's Wort to help keep serious attacks of sadness away. Now, I'm not suggesting you take as many supplements as I do, but you may find that a few carefully chosen ones will help keep you functioning well physically, which helps you magickally. Visiting a good naturopath is a good idea if you think you need to take supplements. I studied nutrition in my early twenties so I feel confident in self-medicating.

I also keep my coffee intake down and instead drink a lot of rooibos tea. My good mate Dannii Minogue (Kylie's little sister and a singing star in her own right) introduced me to this wonderful tea, which is indigenous to South Africa. She is a health nut and knows all the cool stuff! It's delicious as a late-night beverage. Whenever I stay with Dannii in London we always have a cuppa together before bedtime. By the way, if you check out photos of Dannii you will see she is stunning in all her photos. Well, that's exactly what she looks like when she wakes up in the morning: really fresh and bright eyed, and she puts it down to not drinking caffeine and eating a pure diet consisting of mostly dairy-free vegetarian food.

Life is often so stressful, and sometimes the causes of stress are insidious. Consciously relax by paying attention to your posture (especially when you're sitting at a desk). If there is any tightness in your shoulders or back, take a deep breath and "let go" physically. In fact, I just did it myself! I've been sitting down, writing this book all day, and I have been getting very stiff. And when my body gets stiff, so does my mind.

Regular massage is also a wonderful way to stay well and relatively stress-free—it stimulates lymph flow (which is very cleansing) and is calming and fortifying. My one indulgence is my monthly massage from a wonderful woman here in L.A., Julie Watson. She comes to my house and sets up in my bedroom. First she puts a heat mat on her massage table and a sheepskin throw over it. I lie down and she kneads and gently pummels me all over for an hour and a half, and then I just roll into bed and fall asleep. It really is the best!

Another bonus is that massage not only stimulates and soothes you physically, it also works on your subtle energy centers. When the "chi" life force flows vigorously, as it occurs during the deeply relaxed state that massage creates, your psychic and visualization skills are enhanced, and these are most important for magickal prowess. If money is an issue, consider doing a "swap" with someone. I have swapped lessons on how to cast a circle and other witchy skills for massages—it's a terrific deal!

Every morning upon waking, before performing my coven dedication ritual, I do some simple yoga movements. I bought a good-quality yoga mat, and as I have done classes on and off for years. I have quite a few moves committed to memory, my favorite being "Sun Salutation." My goal in these opening moments of each day is to center my mind and get limber and "awake" in my body, fully appreciating its magnificent design and capabilities and to connect with a strong sense of spiritual focus to guide me through the day. I only spend ten minutes in linear time but it feels as if time stops as I perform the mudras and poses, sometimes listening to evocative music like the soundtrack from the movie *Paris, Texas* or anything by the Icelandic band Sigur Ros.

Good Behavior

In addition to meditations and magick rituals that you may undertake as part of your Witchcraft and coven work, there are other ways you can enhance a peaceful and empowered mind so that you really develop your personal magick. A really easy way to achieve this "vision meditation" is to simply walk or drive somewhere that has a great view, get out of the car, turn off the mobile phone and sit there and enjoy the scenery for twenty minutes or more. Or perhaps find a book that has really lovely images in it, put on some relaxing music, and just enjoy the photographs or drawings.

Consciously calming your mind with peaceful, enriching images and sounds is very healing and helps put you in a better place to do your Witchcraft.

Staying positive is important, as your thoughts control your feelings. If you stop and listen to your thoughts, you may be surprised to discover how negative they often are. Replacing negative thoughts with positive thoughts will help you deal with stressful situations more calmly. I have to constantly monitor my thoughts—I have so much on my plate that sometimes I get really run down and worn out, and start to see only the problems and difficulties in life. When this happens I light a white candle, burn some lemon or clary sage essential oil in a diffuser, and meditate on what is good and positive in my life. Sometimes I will also email my coven sisters and ask them to light a candle for me or send me some energy.

Spoiling yourself is always good. Surround yourself with nice things: burn delicious incense or essential oil candles so that everything smells wonderful and is blessed by the glow of fire; lie naked on a soft rug just because it feels good. Take some time every day to just do slow, sensual, delicious things, live in the moment, and don't think about anything or anyone else—just you and how good you feel.

Turn Off the TV!

Keep your personal space pure and a retreat from the calamity of the outside world. Don't come home from work or school and immediately turn on the idiot box. Instead put some cool music on, light some candles, and spend a moment meditating at your coven shrine. Let magick empower your life in every moment and way possible.

Is It Too Late to Heal?

How do we live as Witches in an increasingly violent world? Well, first we should ascertain if the world really is becoming increasingly violent or if it is just propaganda being happily peddled by the media to keep television news show ratings going up and the advertising dollars coming in.

If you look at the facts, violence is actually on the decrease in our sub/urban societies. Try doing this: go to a search engine website like Yahoo! or Google and type in "violence is decreasing," and see how many links come up stating that, contrary to media reports, violence is on the decrease.

Here's a bit of homework. Don't watch the news and don't buy into the war-mongering and fear that is promoted by the media to sell advertising space. When I started writing this book, the Bush government had declared war on Iraq. Since then I have deliberately not watched the sensationalist news reportage on television. So far, I've only caught glimpses of it at the gym (from the televisions scattered around), but I quickly avert my gaze. I was alarmed when I went in to have a meeting with my television agents (who are packaging and shopping around the television show I am developing here) and they were talking about how the overwhelming consensus amongst TV viewers is that the war is not entertaining enough; to quote, "We want to see more explosions and stuff!" My agents were saying that everyone is so desensitized from the onslaught of reality shows like *Fear Factor* and *Survivor* that they have a hyper concept of what is "real." Really real is just not enough anymore.

I only listen to local and international public radio for accurate, non-sensationalist reporting, and I light candles at night praying for healing and a quick end to the fighting. I'm also conducting public rituals for healing and peace for all life on this planet.

As a coven, do what you can to promote positive thought and healing in everyday life, not just when you are gathered together in circle. Conduct yourselves responsibly and with the awareness that not only your actions, but also your thoughts, contribute to the way the world manifests.

Environmental Magick

Simple, small acts of kindness add up to large shifts in consciousness. A great place to start being kind is to the environment.

Humble acts of environmental awareness can save forests. For example, how many of us throw away a ton of paper at work or school every day? Printing and photocopying errors mean tons of wasted paper. Now you might say, "My office/school has a recycling program," but imagine if you used the other side of the paper, either as notepaper (to save using note pads) or to print out drafts of essays or reports for you to review and edit. Basically you would be cutting your paper waste in half. Don't worry, there is still plenty of paper to be recycled! But even recycling efforts cannot cope with the incomprehensible amounts of paper that are used and wasted every day in the world. When I discuss recycling with people they often say, "But what effect will my actions have when so many other people don't bother?" I answer that it will affect them—making a change for the better by consciously acting responsibly improves your individual attitude, and that's worthwhile enough for a start.

Another way to really practice what you preach is to drive an environmentally friendly car. Living in L.A. and having to drive all the time makes me very conscious of the amount of smog and noise that even one car generates. Along with Tom Hanks, Cameron Diaz, Leo DiCaprio and a bunch of other environmentally conscious celebs, in L.A. I drive a hybrid car: part petrol-powered, part battery-powered. Mine is a Toyota, but more and more car companies are developing similar types of cars. You will cut smog and noise by half (the car switches to electric when you pull up at a red light and the engine becomes silent—it's cool!). And you don't have to "plug it in" to charge it up. The car runs on a little bit of fuel and the battery charges itself. It truly is the best car for a cleaner future.

Stop saying "It's too hard" and "I'm only one person, what difference can I make?" As much as I advocate being your own boss, I'm telling you (!) that those two sentences are not allowed in a Witch's vocabulary!

Never throw your hands up in a futile manner, saying "The destruction of this planet has gone too far; the tide can't be turned—it's not worth it." Instead, start saying "I'm here right now, and I'm worth it." That's true witchy thinking. A real Witch is self-absorbed in the most positive of ways, because s/he knows that the world will answer according to the questions asked of it, and that they need to be of fit mind, heart, body, and spirit to ask the best questions. The more Witches see hope and goodness, the more hope and goodness there will be.

Community Service and Environmental Activism

An important part of coven homework is serving the community and working to heal and protect the environment outside of their immediate circle. For example, community service can mean helping out with youth crisis services. I recently spent every Monday for six weeks teaching a group of troubled teens about positive action, both practical and magickal. It is a really good discipline for you as a coven to commit to at least three community service programs a year.

Environmental activism can take the form of practical action, like taking part in marches, planting trees, sponsoring an endangered animal or joining Project Aware, Oceania, Planet Ark, or Greenpeace. Visit my website for links to environmental action sites in the "Gaia Gateway" section.

Another important part of caring homework is to only buy environmentally friendly cleaning products, recycled paper and plastic products where necessary, and basically practice what Witches preach: that nature is sacred and worthy of the utmost respect.

A Final Note on Home Coven Disciplines

If you are serious about contributing to the coven you are a part of, you will most likely spend quite a bit of your time at home studying up on the Craft. Maybe you will be undertaking a Witchcraft 101 course and creating spells, rituals, poems, and odes to the Goddess for your coven's Book of

Shadows. You may be recording your personal thoughts and magickal revelations in your own Book of Shadows. Each morning you will be performing your coven dedication, and every moment of your life will be imbued with a magickal mindset as you grow stronger as a Witch, nurtured by the relationship you have with your coven, both in this world and the worlds in between.

Witchcraft 101

In a traditional coven, an initiate is generally put through a course of formal education. This course may take the form of certain books they are told to read and then are quizzed on by the coven's high priestess in the form of sit-down tests and examinations. They may also be given a copy of the coven's Book of Shadows to study. Generally this period of learning is called "First Degree Initiation" and is for the period of a year and a day.

When you are starting your own eclectic coven, it is a really good idea to have a course of formal study, so that you are all learning together. Some of you, of course, will know things that others don't and may feel like you're going over old ground—but a bit of revision never hurt anyone! I do it all the time. I love re-reading my old books and exploring new theories and ideas as I experience the evolving spirit of the Craft.

In offering the following course guide, I hope to help you create a study structure for the greater growth and good of your coven or your working group, as this structure can also work very well as preparation for forming a coven. The course structure provides guidelines on what sort of information you should familiarize yourselves with, arranged in an order of subjects that enables you to understand more complex magickal tasks and theories as you progress.

A year and a day may seem like a long time to be an initiate, but it's actually very short as far as time required for personal development and a "wisdom" shift. What a Witch knows isn't just about the information your rational brain has a handle on, but it also concerns inner knowledge, intuition, and psychic abilities that will evolve within you as you put that information into practice.

In Witchcraft, the really important stuff is not so much the accumulation of facts and figures and formulas but is more about a shift in consciousness, where the self awakens to a greater sense of evolutionary purpose and potential in every aspect of existence—physical, mental, emotional, spiritual, and magickal. Rather than designing this learning experience so that it runs for a year and a day, I have created an eight-part course. If you were really committed and pretty good at absorbing information, you could probably cover this in eight weeks. Ideally, though, I would recommend you spend at least two to three weeks studying the lessons of each part of the course, with a fourth week being devoted to a series of practical exams that the coveners take part in, "grade," and discuss together.

So if you are a Witch who is hungry for knowledge, ready to work, and committed to achieving positive results, read on!

The lessons in each part should be structured around the themes and concepts below and can include:

- The lessons themselves, researching information and writing up a personal report.

- Practical and magickal exercises to develop the necessary magickal skills—for example, blending incense, making a money spell, or reading tarot cards.

- A circle gathering/ritual to assist in absorbing the knowledge spiritually as well as intellectually.

- An examination of sorts or a discussion to share knowledge and see if everyone, or perhaps just a newcomer who is doing the course, is ready to progress to the next stage of initiation.

A Guide to Creating Your Own
Course in Witchcraft

Again, below are breakdowns of the kinds of topics you should be studying. You will notice that I have not included all the required information here—that would be another huge book in itself. Most of what I have suggested looking into is either in my earlier releases or in the books I have included in "Recommended Reading" at the end of this book. The best way to approach creating your own course is to choose various books, magazine articles, and Internet articles that cover the topics below and either photocopy or print out what you decide is the best material. By doing this you can put together your own Initiation Course Handbook, so that people joining your coven later on will be able to benefit from your initial hard work, having their study material all mapped out for them!

Of course, your learning and development in a coven will not rigidly adhere to the outlines below. If, however, as a formal part of your training you attempt to do the lessons suggested below in addition to the general goings-on of coven life, you will find your personal craft will really develop in a satisfying and empowered way.

The Course

Part One

What a real Witch is: Address the misconceptions and educate yourselves on the myths and fallacies as much as the realities, so if you are confronted by people who have false ideas you can educate them with empathy and compassion.

Living Witchcraft: Read up about how other people live it, do it, and be it, and learn from their examples.

The three laws of Witchcraft: Analyze these and think of practical examples of how the laws could be applied. Consider the deeper lessons behind the laws—namely, that Witches take responsibility for what happens in their lives and know that in order to change the world to be more to their liking, they must start by changing themselves.

The past story of Witchcraft: How we got to here. Make sure you include some study of ancient Pagan religions, religious persecution of Witches throughout the ages (including the Burning Times), as well as the more recent expressions of the Craft like Gardnerian Witchcraft right through to the current explosion of interest in Wicca in the Western world. The past story of Witchcraft is very much a "fill in the blanks" affair. So much information has been corrupted and destroyed, so don't be too pedantic about what you try to absorb. Personally, I always feel more empowered and more of a sense of community and belonging when I focus on where the Craft is now and where it's heading. But having a reasonable idea of the role that Witchcraft and magick have played in the evolution of civilization is an important part of personal empowerment as a Witch.

Part Two

The Witch's tools of magick: The athame, wand, chalice, pentagram, cauldron, Book of Shadows, altar, candles, etc. Now is the time to study and understand the significance of the pieces of your magickal arsenal. If you haven't already, now may be a good time to go and procure these items and consecrate them. It's also a good time to look into special garments like magickal robes and sacred jewelry, if that's your style.

The science of magick: How it works, both physically and metaphysically. I always think it's important to think and act practically as well as magickally, and understanding the science of magick helps you anchor your rituals and spellcasting so that they are really effective.

Casting a sacred circle: Creating a sacred space in which to do magick and learning how to invoke and work with the four elements of magickal manifestation: air, earth, fire, and water. If you haven't already, now is the time to learn how to cast a circle, and an important part of this is understanding the qualities of the elements to help you invoke them more powerfully in the circle.

Part Three

Divinity and personal power: Research the goddesses and gods, both ancient and modern, and how they are created and how to interact with the various forms and archetypes that they manifest within. Practice meditation and visualization to connect with divine presence and personal power within. Study up on how to raise the power of the gods to fuel your magickal work by raising the cone of power and working with this energy.

Sex magick: Understanding sex magick and using orgasm as a sacred energy source to be used in magick is empowering. Obviously this is only for people who are older and sexually active, though I think it's healthy and appropriate for teen Witches to have an appreciation and love for their bodies and sexuality, and an understanding of the sacred nature of orgasm.

Part Four

Full Moon Rituals: The essential monthly ritual of honoring the moon is called an esbat. Also, the magickal potentials of the waxing, waning, and dark phases of the moon should be studied.

Everyone should make themselves very familiar with the myth of the wheel of the year and the eight sabbats, or Witches' holy days:

Samhain: The Festival of the Dead and Witches' New Year.

Yule: The longest night and Witches' Christmas.

Imbolc: The awakening of spring and the Festival of the Maiden.

Ostara: Spring Equinox, day and night stand equal, and the Festival of Youth.

Beltane: May Day, a fertility festival.

Litha: The longest day and the peak of summer.

Lammas: The first harvest.

Mabon: The second harvest.

Part Five

Spellcasting: Before you start doing spells together, it's important to understand the process of them so that you are connected emotionally and spiritually to your efforts. It may be worth revising your magick and science lessons here, because when quantum physics talks about the world manifesting according to the way it is observed, it could be talking about spellcasting and how to create form from will.

How to create spells: Include examples of love, health, prosperity, and healing spells; you should all make up your own once you have a good comprehension of how they work.

Witchcrafting skills: Blending magickal incenses and oils, washes, powders, and making charms. This can be fun and like a big cooking lesson! Tasks like blending incenses and mixing herbs and magickal powders to put into spells and charm bags can be easily shared. Learning the properties of crystals, stones, and other sacred objects and how to use them magickally is also an important part of honing your spellcasting skills.

Part Six

Dark magick: Notice I say dark magick, not black magick. We're not talking about evil, we're talking about the darker, more difficult experiences in life that are really the stuff from which our character and personal power are forged. Following are areas that despite their intense and sometimes confronting undertones are very positive to educate yourself in:

Psychic attack: How to protect yourself against it.

Hexing: The role it plays in Witchcraft.

Binding and banishing: How to stop people from hurting and exploiting others.

Death, destruction, and decay: Honoring and respecting these events as essential to life.

Mortality and eternity: What happens when we die.

Part Seven

Special skills: This section can serve to introduce individuals to the various specialist skills they may choose to explore as a Witch, like astrology, divination, tarot or tea-leaf reading, and other psychic skills.

Understanding symbols and omens: Research the meanings and origins of omens and symbols that we use in magick.

Dream work: Understanding dreams. Everyone should keep a dream diary for at least the period of this lesson and analyze their dreams as a part of their study.

Astral projection: How to leave your body with focused and specific meditations. You may also like to explore making ointments and potions that assist in out-of-body experiences.

Part Eight

Rites of passage: Milestones in a Witch's life, including first orgasm, first menstruation, first sexual union, childbirth and baby blessings (similar to christenings), Maiden/Mother/Crone and Youth/Father/Wise Man life-passage rituals, and handfasting (a Witch's wedding—for a year and a day or as long as love lasts). All these rituals should be studied and understood and, if it is appropriate, perhaps some may be performed at this time.

Personal magick: Putting it all together and living the life of a Witch, including personal habits like healthy and responsible eating, environmental conservation, and treading lightly on the planet. If you're not already looking after yourself and the planet, now is the time to start. Everyone should join an environmental conservation organization and make a donation in the name of the coven.

Pagan pride: Take action to encourage respect and tolerance for Witches and Pagans. Go out into the world empowered and proud.

So there you go! There's a lot to learn, but you have a lifetime if you choose. I have found over the years that I will learn something at a surface level, but as the years progress my comprehension becomes deeper and more profound and I cease to "remember" things: instead, I just "am" these things.

So take your time and enjoy this process, being as creative and imaginative as you desire. And remember, a lot of the time there won't be "right" and "wrong" answers as much as simply people's different opinions and experiences, which should be respected and encouraged as they will create a fertile environment for your coven to grow and evolve.

Reaching Out

Reaching out is something I do a lot of, being out in the media so much. It is something I'm comfortable doing. Having worked in the entertainment industry for twelve years before coming out of the broom closet and talking about my Witchcraft in public, it wasn't too hard for me to adapt my established communication skills of talking about my band or my TV show into talking about my books and the Craft.

Some of you, however, may not feel as comfortable talking about your craft. And, indeed, there is no need to ever mention it outside of your fellow witchy community—in fact, I generally advise against it unless you are directly asked by someone. Creating a positive image for Witchcraft and covens in the general community can be a very rewarding and constructive activity, though. Certainly, you can do a service to the Craft if your intent is to dispel the negative Satanic and "black magic" associations with Witchcraft and let people know that we are here to help, heal, and work for the good of all.

Reaching out has seen me doing countless radio, newspaper, and magazine interviews and TV appearances, like discussing modern Witchcraft with Tyra Banks on her talk show and performing prosperity spells on Los Angeles KTLA's 5 *Morning News Show* and sharing love spells with Ryan Seacrest on his radio show. I have explained the real meaning of Halloween on *Good Day New York* surrounded by kids dressed up as ghouls and ghosts, and had the audience of Lisa Rinna and Ty Treadway's talk show, *Soaptalk*, clapping and stamping their feet to raise energy for a passionate Valentine's Day!

After my appearances, I am always inundated with requests for more information from audiences, the production crew, and the show's hosts. It just goes to show that there really is a lot of positive interest out there!

Can You Do a Spell for Me?

If someone directly approaches you for a spell, it can be considered reaching out because (if you decide to do it) you are opening up the practices of the Craft to others. I do a lot of spells for others: the problems I am asked to help with range from helping people repair marriages, sell houses, and get better jobs to general blessings for good fortune. The sadder ones are requests to help those who are sick or dying and are not feeling at ease about their transition. I never advertise my services, though; if someone approaches me for help, I see it as fate that has drawn us together, and it is my duty and privilege to help. I never charge money. When the spell or ritual works for them, I ask them to donate money or their time to charity. I would advise you to do the same. I do not think it is appropriate to charge money for services like this. For a start, it makes it difficult to guarantee the spell will work. Also, if you do not charge you will have the person's complete trust and faith in your sincerity and your power, and it is this energy of theirs that you need to fuel the spell with so that it will manifest the desired result.

When I do spells for people like this I have absolutely excellent results—pretty much 100 percent success—because I have 100 percent of the recipient's belief. In situations like this, we are acting in service to the greater good, and that brings its own rewards. It is important, though, that the recipient does give something to share their good fortune. If it is not money, then they should donate some of their time or services to a worthy cause.

We're Here, We're Witches—Get Used to It!

Public displays of Witchcraft that are beautiful and fun definitely have a positive effect on the way people see us, so why not consider holding open circles and sabbat celebrations in your area?

If you are setting up a public ritual from scratch yourself, make sure you get official city council approval beforehand. Contact your local city council and explain that you would like to hold a spiritual meeting on public land; alternatively, sign up to be part of one of the established Pagan festivals happening frequently around the country. Visit the websites and contacts at the back of this book for more information.

If you are organizing a meeting or celebration yourself and want to let the community know about upcoming activities, why not post a notice in your local organic food co-op, at your local Pagan/New Age bookshop, or anywhere you think like-minded people may congregate? Make sure when you do the event that you have some sort of security organized (like any public event), and make sure lots of your own friends are participating so that you have plenty of support! A public gathering can be an elaborate event, almost like a theatrical show, or it can be a simpler affair. I conducted a relatively spontaneous public ritual recently that had an attendance of about sixty people. Eleven were known to me and the rest were interested (and luckily mostly respectful) strangers. It was part of a small festival with council approval. The Witches and I were going to demonstrate a circlecasting; however, the spectators wanted to join in, so we created a double circle (one smaller circle of people surrounded by a larger circle) with the experienced Witches scattered throughout the public participants.

We cast the circle together, with me calling clear instructions; for example, "Face east as we call on the element of air. Close your eyes and feel the breeze on your face, smell the scent of our sacred incense, and concentrate on how the winds of change bring new beginnings and new energies. Repeat after me: We call on the element of air!" It wasn't the type of quarter invocation that I would normally use, but I tell you what: with sixty people thinking about air in this way, the element manifested itself most convincingly in our sacred space. And it was the same for the other quarters.

When I invoked the Goddess and God, I asked everyone to think of something they liked best about themselves, and it was in that wordless moment that a profound sensation of love and joy filled our space. It was truly the energy of the divine! Then, once the circle was cast, I asked that everyone close their eyes and focus on something they really wanted to come to them, to have a very clear vision of it. I then said to join together in raising power by clapping and stamping along to a chant that I called. In this way we raised the cone, and at the peak I called out the seal of intent:

> The vision is real
>
> The magick is sealed
>
> For the good of all
>
> With harm to none
>
> Our will be done
>
> Our will be done.

On the second "Our will be done," most of the crowd intuitively joined in repeating this, and the seal of intent was indeed confirmed. Then I invited everyone to send a hug and kiss around the circle with a wish that "Thy will be done." Everyone focused on letting any excess energy drain through their feet into the earth as I opened the circle. It was a fantastic ritual that was very easy to do, and the effects were enormous. So much positive energy and goodwill was shared that I was still on a high from it the next day. When your coven is comfortable and confident with performing rituals together, consider opening the doors to your crafty life and letting others enjoy the view!

Let's Get Political

You can engage appropriate use of political activism to protect the rights of Witches to practice their craft. In America, a major breakthrough in Witches' legal right to practice was when the U.S. military chaplain's handbook was adapted to include Wicca. The Covenant of the Goddess, an international affiliation of Witches and Pagans, was instrumental in campaigning for this to occur.

There are laws in America that prohibit discriminating on the basis of a person's religion, but every day there are still struggles for acceptance and respect. The best way to deal with ignorance is with patience and compassion through gentle education. However, sometimes more active consciousness-raising is appropriate, whether it be (peaceful) public demonstrations, emails to government officials, or collecting signatures to create awareness of religious freedom issues. If you are a practicing Witch it is quite likely that you have already had a hand in environmental activism, so consider also turning your skills to working toward more tolerance and acceptance for Witches. The best place to start is to contact the Wiccan and Pagan organizations featured in the contacts section and ask them what causes or action they are involved in. If you see something that needs addressing, then in turn enlist these organizations' help.

A Final Word

Witches don't proselytize, and none of the above suggestions should involve preaching. But consider this: if there is one witchy responsibility that could be seen as a little like preaching and extends out of our immediate circle, it is this—to keep people aware of all the good things in life, sharing the idea that heaven is here on earth. So educate those who would throw up their hands and say, "What's the point of caring about the environment and each other and finding magick in the world? It's going to ruin!" Let them know that violence is on the decrease in our communities, that environmental issues are being addressed, and that positive progress is being made. Organic and sustainable crop and animal farming methods are increasing and are humane and healthy for us and the planet; recycling is mandatory in most giant corporations; alternative energy sources are being developed, and hybrid cars are the way of the future—there is hope for our species! As the war in Iraq rages on while I write this book, I'm focusing on the outpouring of wishes for peace and love that circle the globe, which remind me of what is honorable and brave in the human spirit. It is this expression of the human spirit growing wiser and enlightened that will guarantee us a relevant place in this biosphere for the future.

Put some positive reinforcement out there. People will feel more compelled to take action in their everyday lives because they are being encouraged to see that an individual can make a difference. Our smallest thoughts and actions really do add up to create the world in which we live. As a Witch, preach love, preach strength, and share the magick of our craft!

appendices

The Elements of Me
Tri Johns

I have to always be a warrior and battle to be respected and acknowledged in this world as a woman, as an African American, and as a Witch. But combining African American and Witch together—well, that creates an unusual kind of war. I must admit, it's a bit unnerving to use the term "African American Witch," knowing that in parts of Africa today women are still hunted and killed even if they are merely accused of practicing Witchcraft. Time hasn't changed in those parts of Africa. Mournfully, time has stood still. Though we are not hunted and killed here in America, it is still a struggle to live life with an unwavering conviction. There's a general brainwashing, an implanted fear that comes over most people; fear of being true to their beliefs and true to themselves; fear of anyone who stands by their own ideals. I've made my decision. I will be true to myself. I won't succumb to the "normal" and "general" practices that most have accepted. I've decided to own my life and live completely unto me. I own who I am. I own my strength as a woman, I own my pride as an African American, and I own my courage as a Witch. I am an African American Witch.

Tri Johns is an African American Witch living in L.A. and one of the founding members of the Dark Light of Lilith coven.

Up until now, I have lived my life as an African American Witch in a somewhat private existence. Though I am featured in a few books on the topic of Witchcraft, my family does not know of my beliefs, nor do my friends. Being so secretive instills a sense of loneliness at times. I have concerns of being even more isolated if those souls who are close to me knew of my beliefs. Sometimes I think my solitude is by ancestry design so that I am inclined to observe my craft, augment my wisdom, and bolster my power. I have told a few unfamiliar persons about my practices just to stimulate their reaction. My thought process was that if an absolute stranger could be disposed to appreciate my beliefs, then I know my friends and family would be even more accepting. So when I begin to converse with a stranger, I usually start with a comment about the moon. This lets me know how much I can tell this person. If they respond with a positive comment, then I can tell them everything. It's compelling to watch the myriad reactions, but at the same time the responses have left me feeling unfulfilled.

It has been my experience that because I am African American and because I believe in Witchcraft, some people automatically assume Witchcraft and Voodoo are one and the same. The Hollywood system has distorted and tainted the tradition of Voodoo so much that people fear the word itself, and because I am African American they tend to consider any ritual-based spirituality that I believe in to be of this imprecise Hollywood depiction. And it's this depiction, of course, that incites the panic. I begin to sense a hint of trepidation and nervousness surrounding those souls I've just hoped to enlighten. I see their eyes change and I know they want to run away as fast as they can but they feel obligated to be polite and stay a little longer. Then, of course, they think of a reason or two as to why they must leave that instant. It's these occurrences that have prompted me, in the past, to feel that I must live a secret life as an African American Witch. Being judged does not trouble me as much as being misunderstood. Witchcraft is its own entity. Voodoo is its own entity. Just because I am African American, the two entities do not become interchangeable. And there should be no fear of either, just respect for each on its own.

Most of the unfamiliar people I have approached with the topic of Witchcraft were African American. Interestingly enough, they are the ones who withdrew their energy the fastest. I've pondered the situation to grasp the reasons as to why my African American brothers and sisters shut down so quickly. I believe that just the mention of any ritual-based spirituality strikes a chord deep within African Americans, and on some level it becomes familiar to us. We are connected to our ancestors. Subconsciously, these African American brothers and sisters knew what incredible power resides in rituals and how they can be quite tangible. Their first instinct is to provide no energy to the thought. They shut down immediately. They do not want to ignite the power within themselves. They do not want to go to a place where they can feel the surge of their ancestors' energy and the potency of the practices their ancestors believed in, as if feeding these thoughts would bring forth visions of harrowing rituals and pull them into a world that is much too vigorous for the American side of them to handle. I, as an African American woman, know these qualms well. I too had inklings of them in the past. I learned to embrace them and allow the power to be. I've allowed all energies to flow freely and settle in their time. So I do understand my African American brothers and sisters who shy away from just the thought of Witchcraft. I just had anticipated seeing more evolvement with time.

I see elected spirits of my ancestors in my visions. They come to me daily. I see them just as I close my eyes. They are performing a ritual. They're all dressed in white fabrics that are draped around their bodies and white turbanlike hats on their heads. It's only the women I see, and they emerge like goddesses. They are all African and they encircle me. They dance around me, smiling, rejoicing and embracing every part of me. I feel the love emanating from them. I feel so honored to be in their presence. This vision of adoration is a daily assurance that I am on a chosen path. I am meant to be an African American Witch. I welcome the day that my American Indian ancestors grace me with their presence as well. I embrace all of the parts that make up who I am.

Though this spiritual phenomenon had always been an amazing ethereal support system, I still longed to be a part of an influential sisterhood on this physical plane to share magical experiences with. I longed to be in a coven.

When I often visualized myself as a member of a coven, I was always at the creative core. I wanted to be a part of its conception. My visions are very sharp, and I constantly cultivate my skills. I desired to be part of a group with comparable ability and discipline. I was quite aware that going into an already formed unit would mean having to adapt to their way of crafting. I was open to the idea but it wasn't my heart's desire. I didn't want to be in a coven that was solely African American, for I already have the spirits of my ancestors deeply embedded into my being. I really wanted to be a part of a coven that was diverse in culture and experience. I realized I must allow the proper energy to find me. It could take days, months, or years, but I knew that the timing would be perfect and I would be prepared to recognize its arrival. As the Goddess would have it, I didn't have to wait too long. Once I committed to the decision, all related things fell into place.

We convened on the patio of a local coffee house one sun-drenched afternoon. The instant the three of us assembled around the table, I felt a magnetic energy spiraling around us and flowing through me. My mind was racing. I remember thinking "I aspired to be a part of a supportive sisterhood and here it is before me." It was surreal. I was guided to Fiona, and unwittingly acting as a conduit, I steered Fiona to Zorrita. The circle of energy was complete and the connection was extraordinary.

To reassure ourselves that we would not forego the opportunity to connect with another amazing energy, we did a brief search to add a fourth individual to the initial core of the coven. It was not meant to be. Our energy was so incredibly familiar that our search was futile. This pursuit confirmed our primary instinct that our core coven must consist of just us three. So we devised a plan to add others to our circle in the future.

I was very excited and passionate about this new venture. I practiced my craft vehemently and was very passionate about continuing to hone my skills as a Witch. But drifting in my mind was a lingering thought, one prevalent desire: I yearned to have one special goddess who always made her presence known in my life, a goddess who would always provide encouragement. Of course, one can ask any goddess for her guidance, but I wanted a personal connection to one specific goddess that would be as meaningful as the connection I have with the spirits of my African ancestors. She didn't have to be African but she had to ignite a secret power in me. I did not want her to be the sole goddess in my life. I just wanted that principal goddess who habitually came to me. I sought guidance from the spirits of my African ancestors, but they left me to find this goddess that I yearned for on my own.

Many goddesses came to me periodically but there were only two who were always present: Kali and Lilith. Kali and I share a sacred day (a birthday) so I presumed that Kali was going to be that one significant goddess in my life. But then Lilith began to emerge. She appeared in my life morning and night. She would fly around in the hidden alcoves of my mind. I could feel with certainty that she was the one, and it became important to me that she be an integral part of our coven.

Our core coven is diverse in experience and rich in culture and ethnicity, just as I had desired. The style is eclectic. And our patron goddess is Lilith.

The very first ritual the three of us performed was captured on film. We briefly discussed the basic structural sequence of the ritual beforehand. We agreed on what we desired the end result to be but we did not scrutinize it. Instead we encouraged our inner voices to free us and guide us collectively throughout.

Viewing the reel allowed us a bird's-eye view of the ritual. It was very poignant to see our interaction from a different perspective. Each juncture was enchanting. The ritual flowed effortlessly and we verbally danced in perfect unison. The smiles on our faces are evident as we marveled at the synchronicity of our gestures. We allowed the collective energy to guide us in the moment and were rewarded with the purity of our exchange. The bond was official. We were a coven.

It is very befitting that our first ritual be captured on film, for we live in the birthplace of Hollywood and I work in the entertainment industry. Being an artist, one always wants to bring about positive change and open peoples' minds, hearts, and ears to the core of something they may not be used to hearing, see something that they may not be used to seeing, or believe in something that they may not be used to believing in. I want to bring about an optimistic change in the mindset of the masses. The complexity of being an African American and a woman in Hollywood speaks for itself, but the struggle of being a Witch in Hollywood has not found its voice. It has its trials but the battle is worth it if it incites a positive change. The challenge for me is not being able to fully express my beliefs and have them represented respectfully in the film medium. I don't want my beliefs or my words turned into another comedic farce or a deep, dark, suspenseful drama purely for entertainment value. My beliefs are important to me and I want to honor them. So I keep my beliefs close to my heart and only at the precise sliver of a moment, in the appropriate situation, will I express them and create something meaningful for the world to appreciate.

It is my vision to bring about constructive change on so many levels, three of which include as a woman, as an African American, and as a Witch.

Living and Loving It
Allyson E. Peltier

My journey with the Old Gods began at the age of nine. I'd always loved fantasy: unicorns, sorceresses, fairies . . . I wasn't sure if they were real, but immersing myself in that culture cultivated a sense of layered reality that there was more to the world if you just learned how to see it. So it seemed synchronistic when a friend lent me a novel about three girls who decide to form a coven. I read it in one day and instantly decided to do the same. Being a bookworm, I went straight to the library to dig up everything I could about "real Witches" so our magic would be more effective than the make-believe in the novel. It's funny that I never questioned the reality of Witchcraft; I only knew that its portrayal in the book was fictitious. One day at the library I found a book that explained that Witchcraft, practiced in a modern form called Wicca, was a legally recognized religion in the United States and had been since before I was born! I now knew what a "real Witch" was and knew I wanted to be one.

For the next ten years, I read every book I could find and practiced what I read. There was no Internet or email at that

Allyson is a longtime initiated member of a coven based in New York City and a high priestess of an international congregation.

stage, and there were no occult shops in my area, so I had no way of meeting other Witches. I tried to interest some of my friends in Wicca, but they never took to it. So I remained a solitary practitioner until I went off to college. As my access to tools and magickal ingredients was limited, the lessons I learned—self-confidence, perseverance, creativity in crafting rituals and spells, and flexibility—all helped shape my character, and I wouldn't trade those years alone for anything. If you are alone, no matter what your age, don't let fear of "doing it wrong" stop you. It's the practices that connect you to the divine and which will fill your life with magick—coven or no coven.

In my sophomore year of college, I finally made contact with the greater Pagan community. I celebrated sabbats with a large local group and met for moon circles with a select group of new Witch friends. Eventually we decided to make it official and form a coven.

The group of us who became circle Amaurot met repeatedly to discuss exactly what we thought a coven should be. We bought a really helpful book called *Coven Craft* by Amber K and used it as a jumping-off point for creating our coven structure, traditions, degree system (representing levels of experience and knowledge), and bylaws. We also did some research on the Internet and asked around to find out what other covens were doing. Finally, we created a tradition that really worked for the ten of us. It was difficult: some of us were very structured, and we butted heads with others who didn't like a lot of rules. But the process of compromise resulted in a really solid base for a practice that had deep meaning for all of us.

Still, as we worked within the frame we had created, we lost a few people. One moved away, another suddenly lost interest. A year later two more left; they preferred working alone and with groups that they didn't have to commit to. A coven is nothing if it isn't that: a major commitment both on a spiritual level and also on a practical one. Running regular rituals requires attendance, leadership, and even funds. The close friendships that evolve in a coven also require attention and hard work to keep them strong—just like any other relationship.

We got together to do crafts, like making candles, and to watch movies or just hang out. We set up an online chat group so we could keep the communication flowing. We argued, pissed each other off, had great fun, and respected each other.

Because we were a "peer group" coven, our structure was different than the traditional model and it was a labor of love that kept us together. We had no one high priest or high priestess to provide leadership, no Book of Shadows to follow. Instead, different people volunteered to create and run each ritual and were thus the acting high priest or high priestess for that ritual. We made decisions through consensus and compromise. We were a very diverse group in terms of skills, level of study and background, so working together made us all more well-rounded. We created an "inner circle" and "outer circle" structure in addition to our rotating high priest/ess-ships because we knew that if we ever expanded there would need to be a distinction in the leadership and decision-making roles. We also created offices and chose officers to handle various responsibilities. I learned a lot about working magically with other people and also about group dynamics. I graduated and unfortunately had to move away, but circle Amaurot still exists and has become a vital part of its local Pagan community. In fact, it runs large public rituals, has taught Wicca 101 classes at the local Unitarian Universalist church, and recently took on a new initiate.

Now I live in New York City, where there are tons of witchy opportunities. I met with two covens before I found the right fit.

The circle of Ara is totally different from circle Amaurot—it is run by a high priestess and has a more traditional hierarchy (though the tradition also includes a fourth degree based on community service and leadership). Six years later, and I'm a high priestess and elder of the Ara Tradition. As we move forward in trying to establish ourselves as a temple, I serve on the Board of Directors and as the editor-in-chief of the newsletter. I actively participate in creating and performing public rituals, help answer mail, and generally assist our president and founder in building our community through workshops, lectures, and services.

My high priestess is very warm and loving, and my other covenmates are all very willing to share their knowledge with me. I am closer to some than others, and unfortunately the group has become a little estranged due to numerous personal difficulties that befell us all at the same time. But the expansion of the temple has afforded me the opportunity to develop relationships with other Ara members who are not covenmates, which has been wonderful. I miss the closeness of my first coven, but I think that has a lot to do with the differences between a group that was formed together and joining one that already exists. There are many lessons to learn from each.

It's very exciting to work in this new structure and be a part of something as important as the forming of a government-approved Wiccan religious organization. I'm also learning new magical techniques with Ara, which is more shamanic than Amaurot. Because our president is a high-profile author and interfaith activist, Ara is very public and is often filmed by various TV stations and interviewed for newspaper articles. I love being able to help bring more information about Wicca to a mainstream audience.

One of the best things about being in a coven is the opportunity to work with group consciousness. It is wholly unlike anything you've experienced on your own and is more pronounced with a familiar group than with any old group at a festival or open circle. It's also great to have people you can turn to when you need a circle called. And with an "activist" coven (like both of mine have been), there are so many great things you can accomplish with a group effort. Covens can do local outreach, participate in fundraising or food-collecting efforts, lead classes and workshops designed to fight negative stereotypes, and much more. When the Temple of Ara is fully formed, for example, we'll be able to raise money to buy a permanent space, provide religious services for laity, and expand our long-distance training program to reach out to those who are living in isolated areas. We'll be a force that continues to fight religious discrimination in the public sphere, improving the mainstream's view of who we are.

Any beginner should be prepared for the rainy days, however. Working with a group means that there are egos involved, including yours. Everyone, even the best-intentioned people, has motives that sometimes clash with others' and sometimes blend perfectly. There are miscommunications, hurt feelings, and sometimes people just change. A coven's health, like a family or any other unit of people, is dictated by the minutiae of relationships. But unlike a family, covens are bound by conscious choice—and you should be willing to make that choice every time you step into a coven meeting or circle. If, every time you walk in, you feel and can express perfect love and perfect trust, then you're with the right group, and the magick you make together will be awesome. Even if you're angry with each other, deep down you must know and believe that you all love each other. Otherwise, you are better off on your own.

Someday I plan to have my own coven, and I know that what I've learned through my individual and coven experiences will help me teach and raise deeply dedicated and magical Witches. I only hope that the community we all continue to build together will keep the lines of communication open, and that it will remember to look beyond the coven to see the incredible number of people all walking similar paths alongside us. We are a widespread, multicultural spiritual tradition with individuals and groups moving alongside one another on like paths, a community that I hope will grow stronger as it grows larger, expanding ever outward as it dances the great spiral of life.

Serene Serene
Serene Conneeley

I am a Witch. For me, being a Witch is more about who I am than something that I do. It's what I believe and how I feel about life, the world, and myself. It's about connecting to the earth, taking responsibility for my actions, realizing the consequences of all I do, choosing to be happy, and recognizing the Goddess and God within all things.

Of course I do things too. I have an altar and a "magic room" of spell ingredients, books, crystals, and peace. I worship the moon and draw strength from the sun. I wish on a lucky star. I dance on a hill with other Witches to celebrate the esbats. I cast spells to let go of pain, fear, and guilt. I draw on the energy of the universe to heal myself and others. I honor the God and Goddess in myself and everyone I meet. (A challenge, I know. Unconditional love is hard, but it's a goal.)

I have been a Witch all my life, but I was formally called that for the first time about ten years ago. It made me smile and burn with a sense of recognition and celebration.

My witchiness was subtle at first. I did Reiki, used crystals, whispered spells to the moon. Maybe I wasn't comfortable

Serene has been a solitary Witch for many years, and recently became a member of a coven.

telling everyone, doing it publicly. People seemed scared of the (mis)conceptions of what it meant. But then, by a series of twists and turns and strange coincidences, I ended up in Peru with a shaman and six other Witches. We did ritual together in the sacred places of an ancient and foreign land, and I felt something within me stir and reach out to these people who also believed those inexplicable things I always had. My Celtic heart woke up screaming and demanded I next go to the British Isles.

I followed my heart and ended up in Glastonbury, ancient Isle of Avalon and place of the priestesses and druids. I impressed a wizard there by making the black clouds part at 4:08 AM on top of the tor, at the exact moment the moon became full. On my next trip I walked around the green fields and mountains of Ireland and danced in stone circles with the spirits of Witches from ages past. I crawled within the womb of the Mother in the Orkneys and climbed the cliffs of Iona in Scotland. Later I wandered along the ley lines of Spain and felt my energy rise and my heart expand. I felt power in exploring the countryside of many nations alone because it gave me the time and space to explore within myself. I felt close to the divine energy, to the Goddess, and then finally the God too, as I connected to the earth and watched the wheel of the year in the turning of the seasons. Now I strive to recapture that in the gray landscape of my city.

I've always been a solitary Witch. When I am alone, I feel my witchiness the most, where I can listen to the divine within. For me, spells are like prayer, a form of gratitude for the life I've created. They are a shaping of intention, a focus of what I want to achieve, a physical expression and way of putting out to the universe my hopes and dreams. I see magic in everything—in a beautiful sunset, in the wind in the trees, in the smile of a stranger, in a frangipani tree in full bloom, in the tiny kindnesses that can make a person's day. I feel magic when I am potting a new plant for my little city garden, when the sun shines on my face, when I get a letter from my sponsor child saying she can now go to school, when I open my heart to someone.

I was a solitary Witch because I crave solitude. Because I am shy. And because I'd never met anyone I wanted to share this part of my life with. But two years ago I went to a public full moon circle and it moved me to be able to share that special time with like-minded people, to be part of something and feel the group energy without ascribing to anyone's ideology or hierarchy. It felt nice to come together with other solitaries and share energy and a mutual respect. It was a set time to do magic, something to look forward to. I smiled at the differences, at some people's theatrics, and applauded as I saw others over time become more confident and hesitantly start to call the quarters. The last time I went I surprised myself by being able to speak when we went around the circle, to say who I was and why I was there. My voice didn't shake. I felt unafraid of saying what was in my heart, confident with these people. It was a nice feeling. I go when I can, but there are different people each time. It's sharing, but without being part of a coven.

Then last year I contacted Suzanne, a woman who was advertising her magickal workshops online, about one of her courses. We started emailing, swapping stories, comparing notes. I met her a few times at workshops—she was the second person in the Pagan community who really inspired me. She doesn't go on and on about her knowledge or her actions, she just quietly does it. She lives her beliefs, does all she can for others, is helpful and kind and giving. So when she invited me to her coven's Mabon ritual I was touched and deeply honored.

I rode the ferry across the harbor as the sun was setting, which was magical in itself, and nervously knocked on the door of an old sandstone building. Someone let me in, and when all was ready on the first floor we climbed the stairs and entered the magical realm. I breathed in the heady smell of incense, the darkened mystery of the room, the flickering candles and four altars set up with magical tools and a sense of reverence. I felt awe in the unexpected and mysterious.

As I was welcomed into the circle and anointed, as I journeyed to the altars and the elements there and was smudged (burnt sage smoke was fanned over me to purify me) and given water and other elemental magic, I was surprised—and happy—that three of the women were the three at a recent Reiki workshop whom I had felt the closest to. This is a group I actually like, I thought wryly: a group without arrogance or condescension. Within their circle I felt welcome, safe, a little nervous about whether I was doing the right thing or not, but always comfortable and relaxed. There was sacred theater of the Persephone myth, and then people spoke about what it meant to them. I didn't say much, because I felt like a guest, and I didn't want to intrude. Silly, I know, but I did feel that I could have engaged in discussion with these women. I felt close to them, to their experiences, even when mine were so different. I knew I could reveal myself, be vulnerable, take part. There was a guided meditation too, and hallelujah, it worked!

Then we raised energy with a spiral dance before collapsing in laughter, and I felt it. There was an electricity in the room, a sense of healing, of shared possibilities and magic that we could take back to our "normal" lives. The circle is open but remains unbroken . . .

We closed circle to begin the feasting, but it still felt like a sacred space. As we passed around the giant goblets of champagne and apple cider, as I talked to the Reiki women and then to others, it still felt like a place between the worlds. Nurturing. Inspiring. Balanced. One of the women asked if I was thinking of joining their coven, and I shook my head, surprised. She shrugged. "It would be nice to see you again," she said.

Then as I took the bus home, and as I lay in bed that night, I thought of the energy shared and the magic we wove and became excited by the possibilities. And suddenly sure that I did want to be part of it. I spoke to Suzanne about my previous hesitations. That, although this sounds awful, I haven't met that many people in the Pagan community that I've felt particularly drawn to. There was laughter at that, because that's partly why she'd formed the coven in the first place. I also explained that I wasn't sure what being part of their coven would involve and how much commitment they would expect. She replied that it was really up to me. They have two levels—a core group who come to all the rituals and a cortex who come when they can. But they like everyone to be involved on some level, whether it's planning a whole ritual or just calling the quarters.

But the thing that really made me feel this one was right for me, and me for it, was that there is no high priest or priestess, no hierarchy. Suzanne is the organizer, but different people take different roles as the need arises. They are eclectic and don't follow a particular tradition. They see themselves as solitary Witches who come together to celebrate the sabbats and full moons, to run a monthly Pagan discussion and social night, but they are more than that. They have formed a place of magic where they can explore areas of interest of any of the coven members, grow together, cast spells, and journey on magical adventures.

There is safety in exploring other worlds with a group you trust. And there is a power in group energy. At the last workshop we cast circle and did a ritual for peace. It was amazing to actually feel the power raised, to sense it, taste it, hold it in your hands. If you decide to join a coven, I suppose the priority—and the hardest thing—is to find the right one, or form one of your own; to be able to connect with the right people. How do you know what you're looking for? I didn't—I didn't even know I was looking. I don't know that it's something you can force or search out. Suzanne said new members usually find them, but I feel that they found me. Magic works as it will, as it should, for the higher good of all. I'm looking forward to bonding with this small group of women, to growing closer, trusting, experiencing the strength of unity, losing my inhibitions. I imagine us sharing experiences, encouraging each other, inspiring and being inspired. I am really looking forward to being involved in the rituals on a deeper level. I am also looking forward to the social aspect of it, to sharing a part of my life with friends who embrace this part of me, who understand the importance of magic. Social celebrations like Samhain and Yule will be fun as well as seriously intentioned. The coven members also do activities like cloak making and belly dancing—fun, adventure, experience, learning. I am also excited that some of them do Reiki, and hope this will give me the opportunity and inspiration to use it more.

Every year at Imbolc the coven has an initiation ritual. Because they see themselves as solitary eclectic Pagans who are members of a coven, the ritual is a reaffirming and/or initiation rite to their own individual path and to another year with the coven. Each person has a turn at being the high priestess and the initiate, making it a beautiful, moving ceremony. I am nervous at the thought, but excited too. I was self-initiated in the mists of Avalon, alone. I'm looking forward to making my commitment to myself and the God/dess with people to bear witness.

I don't think I'd ever felt the desire to join a coven before because until now the public part, the action part, was a smaller part of my life. I didn't act on my witchiness, I just was. But a new friend, who is magical, has inspired me to express myself, and I've realized my friends are interested in what moves me. And as I write this I realize that when I was in relationships I spent less time on myself, on my magic, on creating the life I wanted. It was no one else's fault, but when I was with someone I always hid this part of me, and from myself, too, in a way. Even my closest friends didn't really know what I did, because it was inside me. I wasn't hiding it, I just thought they wouldn't be interested. I had no one to share it with.

All my life I've felt closest to the God/dess in the times when I was traveling alone or living alone. And now that I've been happily single for a while I feel it constantly. I am more confident now. I'm becoming more myself. Through no fault but my own, in a relationship I diminish myself. Hide my true self. Forget about the God/dess within and without. But I am a Witch. Did I not think myself important enough to express? Perhaps. It was easy to let day-to-day life, work, the other person, obligations, take precedence. Now I express my witchy heart with abandon, with faith, with grace.

My readiness to join a coven now corresponds to my readiness to embrace everything that I hold dear. I guess it's like coming out of the broom closet (if that's not what this story is!). It's making a commitment to myself, to the coven, to the God/dess. That no matter what happens in my life, this is important. Magic is important. I am important. I have found my own strength, my own path, my own faith, and that cannot be taken from me. And finally I know that I can share that, build upon it, help and be helped, teach and be taught. I trust that I will be nurtured and challenged in this circle. That I will grow. That the sum of all our glorious parts will be even greater. What can we achieve? There is no limit. The realm of magical possibilities is endless, boundless, immense.

I don't feel that I have swapped my solitary role for being part of a coven—I think you can be both. But I feel that being part of this coven will enrich my magical practice and enrich my life. I hope I help enrich their lives in some way too.

Coven Sutra
Dylan Masson

It was never one of my goals to lead a coven. Life is funny that way. I spent many years as a solitary Pagan following my own path, a path that eventually led me to New England and to the life of a high priest of a tradition of Witches. I set my feet upon that path at a very young age. Between my grandmother's vast personal collections of archeological and mythological reference books and my rather liberal upbringing (think California in the late 1960s and early 1970s), it was almost inevitable that I should be drawn toward magick and the ancient mysteries. It wasn't until my teenage years that I became aware of the fact that there were others like myself (my eternal gratitude goes out to Fiona Zimmer and the whole Greyhaven clan for opening my eyes to the Pagan community). After a number of years in the San Francisco Bay area, I moved to New England for reasons that are best described as karmic.

It was in Providence, Rhode Island, that I would meet my beautiful wife Cheryl, the woman who would become my friend, high priestess, and eventually my other half. She had

Dylan is the high priest of the circle of Salgion and a highly respected Witch who is also the coordinator of the U.S.A.-based action and information group the Witches' League for Public Awareness.

only recently founded the Salgion coven/tradition when we became involved romantically, and after much soul searching, I left my solitary path behind me. At the time, she had another high priest by the name of Gavyn Foxwood, and I was a simple dedicant. A couple of years later, Gavyn moved to New York City and the role of high priest became vacant. The men of the coven took turns filling the role during ritual, and somewhere along the way I fell into the role permanently. The passing of years has seen our humble coven blossom into an entire tradition of covens operating as a legal church. While our tradition has evolved over the years, our underlying structure has essentially remained the same.

The Salgion tradition embraces both the Celtic traditions and the science of metaphysics. We have an initiatory system that includes dedication, three degrees of initiation, and for those who wish to pursue it, a legal ordination within our church. Each of these levels has a minimum of a year and a day before the person can petition for the next one, and it generally takes about seven years to receive a third-degree initiation (each person works at their own pace and is never rushed). Preparation for each level of initiation includes completion of a curriculum that includes reading, classes, rituals, and workshops. When a person joins one of the covens within our tradition, they undergo a dedication ritual in which they take a vow to explore the religion of Witchcraft to see if it is the correct path for them. If after completing the classes, etc., they feel that they are on their correct religious path, a dedicant can petition for a first-degree initiation. The first-degree initiation marks a commitment to the religion. The second-degree initiation marks a commitment to the coven, and requires not only the completion of that part of the curriculum but additional participation in the running of rituals and classes. The third-degree initiation requires a much larger commitment and establishes a person as an elder within the tradition. Many choose not to pursue this level of initiation. To receive a third-degree initiation, the petitioner must make a commitment to the community. As an elder within our tradition, you are expected to serve not only the Witchcraft community but also the community at large. Those elders who have demonstrated a commitment to the community, and have undergone additional training in counseling, legal handfastings (Witches' weddings), rites of passage (memorial services), and other clerical duties are eligible to receive a legal ordination. Once they are ordained, these elders are expected to fulfill all of the public duties offered by every other religion (counseling, hospital visitation, funeral services, weddings, etc.). In addition to these services, these elders are expected to serve as high priests/priestesses of their own covens.

Each of the covens within the Salgion tradition has a unique style that reflects the nature of the high priest or priestess who founded it. My own coven (in addition to the main one that I run with Cheryl) reflects my intimate relationship with the seasons and elements (I wear light clothing all year round—even in subzero temperatures) and iconoclastic nature. As a reflection of my affinity for being in touch with the elements, the circle of Ná Duire works outside year round, in all of the weather New England has to offer. When ice is forming in the chalice or lightning rends the night sky, you get a new appreciation for the cycles of nature. Another characteristic Ná Duiran trait helps to keep me from stumbling into perhaps the biggest pitfall that a high priest or priestess can encounter: ego problems. As a leader of a coven, it is all too easy to let your ego get the best of you. People dedicate into your coven, often with only a basic knowledge of Witchcraft, and to them you are a fountain of knowledge and wisdom. As so often happens, these dedicants will want to put you on a pedestal and treat you like royalty. It might even feel good to be put there (everyone likes their ego stroked, after all), but it will ultimately bring about problems that could tear a coven apart. Eventually, those people who put you on that pedestal will be unable to reconcile your human self, with its human foibles, and the impossible ideal that they have created of you as a coven leader. Feelings get hurt, and covens suffer. Fortunately, I am the leader of an iconoclastic group of people who are only too happy to put me in my place if my ego ever rears its ugly head. As I said at the beginning, it was never one of my goals to lead a coven. But would I give it up for anything? Not on your life!

My coven has become my extended family. We often joke about one's coven being the family that they actually get to choose. I've forged friendships that can never be broken. I've seen the children of coveners grow into young adults. The daughter of one of my initiates has herself joined my coven. These are just a few of the things that I will always treasure from my years as a high priest. As rewarding as it can be spiritually, running a coven, even a small one, requires a great deal of hard work and patience. As a coven leader, you serve as teacher, guide, and counselor to the people in that coven.

When the phone rings at 3 AM and someone is in crisis, you need to be there for that person. When you've had a long day at work and you have a ritual scheduled that night, you can't just tell everyone to stay home. There will always be a class or ritual or spell to put together, but at the end of the day, you will at least know that you made a difference.

Over the last sixteen years, our group has grown from a single coven into a tradition/legal church that incorporates several covens. The troubles and triumphs that our tradition has encountered along its evolution have taught us many very valuable lessons. Here are a few of the most important ones for those who are looking to form a coven:

- Understand that each person in the coven is an individual. Witchcraft is not a religion of masses, but rather one that represents a collection of very independent personalities. Differences of opinion occur frequently within any coven. As a coven leader, it is important to respect the opinions of the other coven members. You don't have to agree with or implement every idea put forth by your coven members, but you should at least be willing to hear them out. Keeping that in mind…

- Don't get so wrapped up in trying to please everyone that you relinquish your control over the evolution of the coven. It is very tempting, especially when you are just forming a group, to go along with every suggestion put forth by coven members. Try to keep in mind your vision for the group when looking to incorporate new ideas. If the idea fits in, then great. If not, maybe it isn't the right time for it.

- Whenever possible, don't let yourself get tangled up in the interpersonal conflicts of coven members. Witches are by our very natures independent. This often leads people into conflict. These conflicts can destroy a coven faster than anything else. In my tradition, we have a simple rule to deal with these kinds of issues: no party in any interpersonal conflict comes into circle until the matter is resolved. If a party requests it, their high priest/priestess can mediate in an attempt to resolve the issue at hand, but we will not side with any involved party.

- Let the coven evolve naturally. Many people feel that their coven isn't succeeding if it is small or doesn't meet as frequently as other covens. Give your coven time to settle into its own unique rhythm. A coven with only three or four members that meets only at the full moon can be just as successful as one with thirteen members that meets weekly.

- Above all, have fun! Forming and running a coven is quite a bit of work. This does not mean that it has to entail an equal amount of stress. Laugh, dance, and enjoy your gatherings. There are times when it is appropriate to be serious, if not downright somber, but at other times a little laughter in circle can lift the heaviest of hearts.

Websites & Contacts

www.fionahorne.com: I am very proud of my official website and for over eight years now I have put a lot of love and time into it to make it the popular and busy site that it is!

In the "About Witchcraft" page you will find general information about Witchcraft and lots of links to international Witchcraft and Pagan groups and suppliers. My "Spell Book" has over 200 spells and also links for international online suppliers and store addresses. "Gaia Gateway" has lots of links to environmentally active groups. Take some time to explore and please enjoy.

Other Websites for Witches and Pagans

There are so many sites for Witches and Pagans—we truly are an online community! Here is information on those featured in this book as well as some of my additional favorites.

Circle of Salgion: www.circleofsalgion.org. This is Dylan Masson's site that is described in his chapter "Coven Sutra." It features a full history of the tradition and description of his coven. You can contact him directly here.

Temple of Ara: www.templeofara.org. As featured in Ally Peltier's piece, the Temple of Ara is a non-dogmatic, progressive, and innovative tradition of Wiccan spirituality based out of New York, but its wings are spread nationwide.

The Witches' Voice: www.witchvox.com. A trustworthy and excellently assembled educational network featuring hundreds of articles, up-to-the-minute news reports of interest to the Pagan and Wiccan community, book reviews, online shopping, and is linked to international contacts. Truly the center of the witchy online universe!

Covenant of the Goddess: www.cog.org. This is an international organization of cooperating, autonomous Wiccan congregations and solitary practitioners. At this comprehensive website you'll find information about the CoG organization and activities, as well as the religious beliefs and practices which comprise Wicca.

www.heartmagic.com: Where you can buy Mermade Magickal Arts' Temple of the Moon Incense. Katlyn is the living Goddess behind this wonderful brand and creates brilliant sacred incenses as well as extraordinary magickal art and sculptures.

mythicimages.com: Oberon Zell's incredible Goddess and God statue images are sold here. This is where I bought "The Millennial Gaia" statue that adorns my altar.

www.2numerology.com: An inspirational Internet site you can use to check numerology correspondences for your magickal workings.

www.sacredsource.com: Where I bought the coven's Lilith statue.

www.lauriecabot.com: The site for my friend Laurie Cabot's business.

www.learningannex.com: The Learning Annex offers terrific educational events nationwide where you spend a night with an instructor being introduced to a topic or skill.

www.riversandtides.org: The site of inspirational artist Andy Goldsworthy.

Witchcraft Publications

newWitch Magazine: www.newwitch.com. This is the best and coolest magickal magazine in the USA for Witches. It reflects the exciting and evolving modern face of the Craft in this country and is a great way to connect with other like-minded Witches and Pagans.

Sagewoman: www.sagewoman.com. *newWitch's* big sister mag and long established as the best Goddess-conscious magazine in the country.

Get Environmentally Active

As I mention above at www.fionahorne.com there is a link, "Gaia Gateway." Go there and you will find links to effective international action groups. The environmental agency I am particularly passionate about is Project Aware Foundation, the diving industries' leading nonprofit environmental organization, which works to conserve the underwater world through education, advocacy, and activism. Visit www.projectaware.org.

Recommended Reading

A listing of my absolute personal faves and those I refer to earlier in this book. When you are creating your magickal library, use this list as a starting point and then let your intuition guide you to the books that are right for you.

Phyllis Curott: The first books I want to recommend are those written by my good friend Phyllis Curott. Her books belong on every modern Witch's bookshelf.

Book of Shadows: A Modern Woman's Journey into the Wisdom of Witchcraft and the Magic of the Goddess (Broadway Books, 1998)

Witch Crafting: A Spiritual Guide to Making Magic (Broadway Books, 2001)

The Love Spell: An Erotic Memoir of Spiritual Awakening (Gotham, 2006)

Amber K: An important and thorough title that will assist you in forming a coven is:

Coven Craft: Witchcraft for Three or More (Llewellyn, 1998)

Scott Cunningham: Referred to in the "Goddess Gatherings" chapter is this lovely book about understanding how to cook not only with sight, scent, and taste in mind but also magick:

Cunningham's Encyclopedia of Wicca in the Kitchen (Llewellyn, 2000)

Janet Farrar, Stewart Farrar, and Gavin Bone: Prior to Stewart's death in 2000, Janet and Stewart had been publishing their works since 1971 and are recognized as experts on Witchcraft and the occult. Gavin joined them in 1993 and has since worked with them on a study of Paganism worldwide, *The Healing Craft*, and *The Complete Dictionary of European Gods and Goddesses* and their most recent, *Progressive Witchcraft*. I highly recommend all their books, including:

A Witches' Bible: The Complete Witches' Handbook (Phoenix, 1996)

The Witches' God, The Witches' Goddess (Phoenix, 1998)

Nevill Drury: Anything written by Australian Nevill Drury is an enlightening read. One of his latest that I love is a complete guide to magick-making with a smart and analytical approach:

Everyday Magick (Simon and Schuster, 2002)

Happily, his original *Pan's Daughter*, the story of Rosaleen Norton, the Witch of Kings Cross, who has been an enormous inspiration to me over the years, has been re-released as:

The Witch of Kings Cross (Kingsclear, 2002)

Antonia Beattie: I know you all want lots of spells, and Antonia Beattie is a champ at coming up with some of the best! Check out her titles:

Power Spells: Magic for Personal Power and Inner Peace (Barnes and Noble Books, 2002)

The Girls Guide to Spells, Antonia Beattie with Amargi Wolf (Barnes and Noble Books, 2001)

Spells to Attract Wealth and Abundance (Barnes and Noble Books, 2000)

Love Magic (Barnes and Noble Books, 2000)

Jessica Adams: An amazing astrologer/living goddess, I always enjoy her work. She has teamed up with two other goddesses to write one of the ultimate guides to modern, inspired living. This is a beautifully presented book and will enchant you with its comprehensive information and advice on astrology, dreams, crystals, energy clearing, numerology, rituals, and psychic power.

21st Century Goddess, The Modern Girl's Guide to the Universe, Jessica Adams,
    Jelena Glisic and Anthea Paul (Allen & Unwin, 2002)

Merlin Stone: This book is a classic read and the title says it all, really. It is an enjoyable insight into pre-patriarchal times when goddesses ruled the earth.

When God Was a Woman (Barnes and Noble Books, 1976)

Disinformation: All titles published by Disinformation (www.disinfo.com) are a worthy read, being brilliant, subversive, outrageous, and life-changing. Check out their titles, including:

Everything You Know Is Wrong, Russ Kick (ed.), 2001

You Are Being Lied To, Russ Kick (ed.), 2002

Book of Lies, Richard Metzger (ed.), 2003

To Write to the Author

If you wish to contact the author or would like more information about this book, please write to the author in care of Llewellyn Worldwide and we will forward your request. Both the author and publisher appreciate hearing from you and learning of your enjoyment of this book and how it has helped you. Llewellyn Worldwide cannot guarantee that every letter written to the author can be answered, but all will be forwarded. Please write to:

Fiona Horne

℅ Llewellyn Worldwide

2143 Wooddale Drive, Dept. 0-7387-1034-2

Woodbury, MN 55125-2989, U.S.A.

Please enclose a self-addressed stamped envelope for reply,
or $1.00 to cover costs. If outside U.S.A., enclose
international postal reply coupon.

Many of Llewellyn's authors have websites with additional information and resources. For more information, please visit our website:

www.llewellyn.com